UN
MASK
ED

BOSS
MEDIA

Manufactured and printed in the United States of America

Distributed globally by BOSS Media
New York|Los Angeles|London|Sydney

Cover design by Cara Showers

ISBN: 978-1-954089-51-8   1 2 3 4 5 6 7 8 9 10

Printed in the United States of America

UNMASKED

CONQUERING SEXUAL SIN AND WALKING IN VICTORY

NEIL GETZLOW

BOSS MEDIA

DEDICATION

Amy, thank you for giving me the ultimate gift in this world . . . forgiveness. Thanks to you (and Jesus) I am transformed.

To anyone reading this story who is struggling behind a mask of sin, it is possible to walk in victory. There is hope. It starts with God.

CONTENTS

INTRODUCTION

My name is Amy, and I am the wife of a recovering addict. Those of you that have loved an addict know the pain of this journey: the sleepless nights, tears, angry conversations, anxiety, and loneliness. You feel like you are the one going crazy while trying to be a detective to figure out what's going on and why your partner is acting differently. I've been in unstable relationships before and knew when it was time to go. But with Neil, I knew the only path forward was to stay and hope for a miracle. God delivered in the most unexpected way.

Unmasked is such a perfect title for Neil's story. He wore the mask of a nice, clean-cut guy so well that you could not see the lifetime of pain lurking underneath. For fifty years, all anyone knew of Neil was that he was your typical "nice guy." He was loyal, hard-working, well respected in his career, had friends and family who loved him, was a great Dad, kept his word, was rarely late to anything, had a great sense of humor and was just the kind of guy I had been looking for my whole life. To the outside world, there was not a crack anywhere to be found on the image he created, but I could see the tiny fractures in his mask start to appear shortly after we got married. And when he finally took off his mask for me, he exposed what I had been fearing for years. He was a broken man, addicted to pornography and sex with other women, and in desperate need of the saving grace of God.

The details of how we got here are not pretty: the lies and betrayal. If I didn't have the strength of Jesus in me, there is no doubt I would have packed up and moved out, leaving Neil alone in his sin. But the miracle of Neil being saved, of our marriage being saved, doesn't happen without both of us being completely broken and rescued by Jesus. That's why I encouraged Neil to share our story. It's a story of hope and a great reminder that it's never too late to find God.

◇◇

I grew up in a Catholic home, and my parents were good to my sister and me. They cared about our education and they tried (sometimes a futile effort) to instill good values in us. We would go to church every Sunday and I did a first communion and confirmation celebrations. I believed in Jesus, but I did not like going to church—I thought it was a good deed and would pay off for me in eternity if I went. So, like a lot people, I only prayed when I needed something.

As a typical curious teenager, I took a detour once I hit high school. God and church were replaced by parties, socializing, and boys. I managed to graduate high school and thought I was a grownup, but I didn't want any of the responsibilities that went with it. I worked just to have enough money to buy clothes and go out drinking with my friends. I moved in and out of my parents' house because I didn't want to follow their rules. They didn't appreciate the fact that I would sleep all day and then work as a server and party all night. I always had fun in the moment but felt empty afterwards.

Shortly after I turned twenty-one, I met a guy and became pregnant with my first son after three months of dating. Even though I knew I didn't want to be with him anymore, we had another son together just one year after my first pregnancy. I was in a terrible relationship with no money and no career. So, what did I do? Well naturally, I met and married an alcoholic and had a son with him before getting a divorce less than eighteen months later.

Neil and I met on Myspace (a social media site that pre-dates Facebook). I was three years removed from a failed marriage. While I was happy living on my own, supporting myself as a hair stylist, and taking care of my boys, I was starting to get lonely. My best friend suggested I get on Myspace to meet someone. I had no idea what I was doing. As I was searching profiles, Neil's came up. I thought he was cute, so I sent him a message that said, "I like tacos, too." That was literally the message. I was so bad at this. I never thought he would respond, but he did.

We started messaging online, then we talked on the phone for four hours and set up time to go to lunch. We hit it off right away. After my previous relationships, it was easy to see why Neil seemed like my perfect match. My friends and family liked him, and his friends and family liked me. We enjoyed the same movies and TV shows, liked the same food, and had a really good time hanging out. So after about a year of dating, we did what seemed like the next step—we moved in together. A few years later, we were married. Then I totally blew up our world.

After Neil and I lived together for a few months, I was at work and someone had left a book called *23 Minutes in Hell* on a table in the break room. The author described in graphic detail his twenty-three-minute experience in hell. I read the whole thing during a slow shift and was freaked out. I came home and told Neil about it. That book had stirred emotions in me that I had not experienced in quite some time, and my religious upbringing kicked in. I wanted no part of going to hell. Unfortunately, Neil wanted no part of hearing about the book and my reaction to it. I thought about it for a few more weeks but then just put it out of my mind.

In the months before we got married, we decided to buy a house, Neil's car broke down, he wrecked my car, and we still had to pay for our wedding ceremony. I repeatedly asked God for help in how to deal with all of this uncertainty but never felt like I got an answer. I kept praying for a sign, for something to lead me. And then a few months after we get married, while driving home from work, I asked God again, "I will follow You, but how do I know You are real?" I instantly felt this overwhelming feeling of love and peace. I don't know how else to describe it.

I started reading the Bible and learning everything I could about Jesus. Of course, I tried to talk to Neil about it, but he looked at me like I had lost my mind. He said, "You can believe whatever you want, but I am never going to follow Jesus." That is the exact moment Neil put on his mask and our relationship began to suffer in ways that I never thought were possible.

I prayed for Neil's soul for eight long years. Whenever he would come upstairs for bed, I would always turn on Ray Comfort videos (if you don't know Ray, look him up on the internet). Ray does a great job of sharing the Gospel with people at beaches across Southern California. Neil would watch for about a minute and then get back to looking at his phone or desperately trying to fall asleep. I know he was thinking that I was crazy and not the same person he married. I could sense that he was questioning whether it was worth it to stay with me. He always said he was happy, but his mood and actions said something different. I never really believed the message would break though, but it did. I am proud of Neil for humbling himself before God and asking for help. It changed our lives.

When I first told my sister and best friend about Neil getting saved and what triggered it, they were naturally extremely skeptical. And rightfully so. I know a lot of women will likely feel the same way after hearing Neil's story.

"How can you be so sure he changed? Once a cheater, always a cheater. How can you trust him again?"

It was not easy to re-build our marriage and trust. The faith-based counselor that helped us through Neil's issues says nine out of ten couples in our situation would have ended up divorced. Neil and I had a lot of tough conversations together repeatedly. I felt like a detective trying to piece together the crimes. I wanted to know every detail from Neil about how he was able to keep his mask on over the years. It hurt listening to the details he shared, but I had to know. We added location-tracker apps to our phones, and I have the password to unlock his laptop and passcode to unlock his phone. He turns them both over to me whenever I'm feeling the need to investigate. Doing those things definitely helped build back the trust. I can go weeks now without feeling compelled to look at what's happening on Neil's electronics.

But the most important thing we did was that we put God at the center of everything we do, and it's been the ultimate blessing.

If you are a woman reading this book, my advice to you if you think your husband or partner is looking at pornography or cheating on you is to trust your gut and call him out on it. Have the discussion. Ask for access to his phone and computer. He will likely deny it but get it out in the open. Don't let it sit in your heart and infect your life. Do whatever you can to unmask it.

If you are a man and need to remove the lust and sin from your heart, put your trust in God and take that mask off. The journey is not easy, but I hope you will see that healing and redemption is possible through Neil's own journey in this book.

Whatever you do, don't look at this as the end of your relationship. It's not. Neil and I are here to tell you that there is hope. It is possible to escape hell on earth and come out with a stronger relationship. You simply must trust the healing power of God. He is truly the Miracle Worker. All glory to Him!

—*Amy Getzlow*

▪ CHAPTER 1 ▪

UNMASKING MY SECRET

"And yet, this man, standing in the midst of nothing, can say, by the miracle of the grace of God, I have been invited into a personal relationship with the King of kings and Lord of lords. In the one way that is truly important, I am rich, I am rich, I am rich."

—Pastor Paul Tripp, Humble Pride, Jan. 20, 2008

I will always remember the night that set my unmasking in motion. It all began Sunday, March 1, 2020 at around 9:30 p.m. I was downstairs in my office working on my laptop, while Amy was upstairs getting ready for bed. My laptop let out a loud *DING*, and my phone hummed as a new text arrived. I grabbed my phone and –WHAM—I got hit with a left hook from God. Here's the message I got: "Hi Neil, you still owe me some money from the other day. You have 15 minutes to send it or I'm going to call your wife." Included with the text was a picture of Amy's Facebook page and her cell phone number.

Immediately I could feel the adrenaline kick in as every cell in my body was focused on survival. That's it—survival. Why? Well, the person who texted me was a prostitute I saw while in Chicago the previous week on a business trip. On the last day of my stay, I got up early before my meetings. It was cold, a brutal north wind was blowing, and the snow was already sticking to the sidewalk—obviously, the perfect time to go for a run and enjoy the beautiful scene in downtown Chicago. But I never made it to my run. Instead of rolling out of bed and putting on my running shoes, I grabbed my phone, found some random website, and started texting women who wanted to trade sex for cash.

I don't know what compelled me to do this that particular morning. I wasn't really needing sex, but my brain just went into auto-pilot mode, and I couldn't stop it. This would be a shocking scenario for most people but not for me. You see, this is how I filled up the giant, empty hole in my heart for more than thirty years. This was my drug of choice. The moment any sign of depression or anxiety would seep into my life (a regular occurrence) I turned to a dangerous cocktail of porn and paying for sex. I was an addict very much like an alcoholic. It was a shame cycle that I couldn't stop. More on that in chapter 4.

After a few texts and no answers, I finally got a response. This person was staying at a hotel within walking distance of me, so I bundled up and set off for my destination. As I approached the hotel, I texted with my "date" to get her room number. Once I arrived at the hotel, the first red flag went off in my head. You needed a key to use the elevator. She wouldn't come down to meet me but instead left the key in an elevator. I spent the next ten minutes waiting for the elevator doors to open and look for the key on the floor. Finally, I found the winning elevator with the key on the floor and headed upstairs.

Once upstairs, things proceeded like any other encounter. We agreed on a price, which I paid through Cash app, and an activity. At that point, I proceeded to undress. As I laid on the bed, she asked if I wanted her friend to join. I said, "Sure, that's fine," again just on autopilot, numb to the whole situation but unable to control it. I paid an extra fee and laid on the bed. The whole time my gut was yelling at me, *Run away, Dummy! Run!* But I just couldn't tell my brain to make it happen. As she started to perform oral sex on me, she kept messing with her phone. It was bizarre and my brain finally started to wake up. I told myself, *Just finish what you came for, and get the hell out of here.*

Well, I may have finished, but my life was about to change forever. As I was getting dressed, a 6'4", 300-pound offensive lineman of a man came out of the other room. This guy could have played for the Chicago Bears. As a 5'10", 200-something-pound weakling, resisting was futile. This was the "friend" that was supposed to join us. He was dressed in drag. He calmly announced, "You're going to have to pay us more money, or we're going to tell your wife." And he turned around his phone to show me Amy's Facebook page.

This was the first time in my life that I actually thought I was about to die. On a side note,, I was already dead in my sin—this would have just ended my life on Earth. It wasn't a bad option at that point. I continued to get dressed and tried to remain calm. At that point, my only thought was to get out of that room. I told him, "No problem, I can pay you more."

Quickly, I grabbed my phone and sent some more cash. Hoping that was enough to get me out of there, I finished getting dressed and slowly walked to the door. The woman then stopped me and said it was her birthday and that I should pay her some more money. Again, I sent more, doing whatever I could to just leave. About $900 later, I made it out of the room and did my best speed-walking to the elevator. As I waited for that oh-so-slow elevator to arrive, a door opened down the hall and I could hear her yell, "You need to send me some more money or we are telling Amy!" *Bing!* Finally, that elevator door opened, I got inside and got out of that hotel.

The cold air and snow felt so good on my face. As I do after every encounter, I promised myself *this* would be the last time I would do something like this. I even laughed it off, thinking I somehow avoided the worst.

But on the walk back to my hotel, my brain was spinning out of control. *Were they really going to call Amy?* I kept rationalizing *There's no way they would call. They are bluffing.* About two blocks away from my destination, I got a text message. It was a picture of me in a very compromising position. That's what she was doing with her phone!

I was obviously freaked out but somehow kept rationalizing it all away. *They won't call. They can't find Amy. They can't find me. Just get out of Chicago.*

Literally ninety minutes after getting out of that hotel room, I was off to work meetings and conducting business. I somehow managed to make it through all my meetings that day and found my way back to the airport to catch a flight back home without anyone noticing that I had just been blackmailed by a prostitute. It still amazes me how I was able to compartmentalize what just happened and go about my day and do my job without even a hint of what was lurking behind my mask.

Now let's go back to Sunday night and survival. Once I got the text, my immediate thought again was, *There is no way this woman is going to call Amy. The moment she calls Amy, she has to know I won't be sending any more money over.* So that was my plan: simply ignore it. Brilliant. For the next fifteen minutes, I paced around my office, trying frantically to Google the phone number for any information or leads I could get on who this woman was, all the while thinking, *No way she calls. No way she calls. No. Way.*

Right as my laptop clock hit 9:45 p.m., I could hear Amy's phone chime a text message alert from the upstairs bedroom. I knew what was about to happen, and I braced myself for impact. About five minutes later, I could hear Amy's footsteps leaving the bedroom and heading downstairs to my office. As each step became louder, my heartbeat grew louder and harder until the door flew open and Amy sprang into my office.

"Are you cheating on me?" Amy asked incredulously. I could see the look of confusion and pain on her face over something on her phone. It was a text message that simply said, "Your husband is cheating on you." As if that's not bad enough, the text included the same incriminating photos that I received on my walk back to my hotel.

The next few minutes were a blur, so I don't have the exact words shared. I blurted out the first things that came to mind. "Yes, I still love you." And "No I don't want a divorce. This is the only time I've done something like this. I don't know why I did it, it was stupid." All the things a guilty person would say to save their marriage. Amy was more angry at this point than anything else. I think that was easier for me instead of having to watch her cry at that moment. That night, I slept on the couch. Around 1:00 a.m., I could hear Amy talking on the phone. She was talking to the prostitute! Thirty minutes later, Amy came down to confront me again. Needless to say, there wasn't any sleeping that night.

I stuck with my story. "This was an isolated incident. I've never done this before. I love you and I don't want a divorce." That last sentence was the only thing I said that was true. After a few days, things calmed down. In my mind, I had survived the worst. The Band-Aid was ripped off, and my life wasn't going to fall apart. Now, that's not to say there wasn't a lot of tears and talking, but I managed to keep my mask intact and avoid telling Amy about this other life I was leading.

Before moving on, I should mention this. Amy and I got married in May 2012. About six months later, she told me she found Jesus and was born again. Let me also mention, I was Jewish by birth and atheist by faith. Jews and Jesus in the modern world just don't mix. For fifty years, I don't think I read one page in a Bible. And that's kind of ironic considering how many hotels I stayed in with a Bible right next to my head in a drawer. Sometimes I would open the Bible but only to see if someone left a stack of twenty-dollar bills inside as a reward.

When Amy and I first met, it was amazing. We went out drinking and partying, enjoying every moment of a secular, sinful life. So, when Amy told me she had found Jesus, I was not very receptive to the message. To be clearer, I legitimately thought she was crazy. No, *seriously*. She even stopped drinking and swearing. We went from having everything in common to nothing at all. I did what any non-believer would do, and over those next eight years, I laughed at her, made fun of her, and often complained to my friends about the changes taking place in Amy and in our marriage.

Now you would think, once you get put in a position like that, you would be scared straight. Unfortunately for me, the story didn't end there. God wasn't done with me yet. I was still trapped in my sin and on the expressway to hell, without question.

About two weeks after the Chicago encounter, God delivered another message, not just to me, but to the entire world: COVID-19. Wonderful! I just confessed to my wife that I was blackmailed by a prostitute, and now we were literally locked down together with nothing to do but talk. I couldn't go get drunk with my friends and ignore Amy, which was something I had gotten very good at over the past few years leading up to this.

As we approached the middle of April, like a lot of people, my anxiety and depression started to reappear. Even though Amy and I started talking more and were working on rebuilding our marriage, my addiction kicked in yet again. I was self-employed when COVID hit, and most of the work I had dried up. I did have a few projects, but instead of focusing on those, I focused on porn. I couldn't go thirty minutes during the day without searching for porn online. Twitter made it so incredibly easy to digest in two-minute bites. Then the other half of my addiction came back. In the middle of the pandemic, I set up a meeting with a woman I had met online that I would routinely pay for sex over the previous nine months: Lola. Why? This was the only way I knew how to suppress my mental demons.

Here's where God stepped in to deliver punch number two. Every time I left my computer, I always locked it. My text messages have always been synced up to my laptop, and there was way too much incriminating evidence in those messages.

On that Monday afternoon, I told Amy I was going to meet my son for dinner and took off. And I did meet him for dinner, but the plan was to meet Lola when I was done. For whatever reason when I left the house this time, I did not lock my laptop, and Amy, already rightly suspicious of my motives, quickly took advantage of the opportunity. She got into my laptop and tried to find her way around the messages even though, as she would admit, she had no idea how to use a computer.

What Amy found was once again shocking—text messages and explicit pictures exchanged earlier that afternoon between me and Lola. Amy managed to figure out how to cut and paste the images and sent them to her phone. She then sent those on to me. As I got to my son's house, my phone lit up. I checked my texts, thinking it was Lola. Instead, I was outed again as being a giant ______(fill in the blank with your favorite noun). I have a few to describe myself that I can't share here, so we will just leave it as "sinner."

I somehow managed to make it through dinner with my son. I didn't eat much, and my son would later tell me I was completely out of it. That twenty-minute drive from my son back to my house felt like twenty hours. What was my story going to be to Amy? How was I going to spin this without her throwing me out of the house like I deserved? And once again, we spent the next twelve hours talking, crying, and fighting.

During this horrible moment, Amy told me I needed to pray to God for some answers. In her mind, this was going to be the only way to save the marriage. In the morning, Amy left the house without a word to go to the grocery store. So, for the first time in my life, I prayed. I told God I needed help and that if He was real, to send me a sign. Ten seconds after I ended my prayer, the garage door opened and Amy was home. Even though I didn't realize it at the time, God was working His will through her, and sending me the help I asked for.

But it was going to take one final gut punch from God for me to *finally* feel compelled to act. Once Amy got home that morning, I told her that I prayed, that I asked for help, and that I thought that help was her. We talked some more that day and agreed to keep working on things. It was about that time that Amy got a random Facebook private message from a guy we did not know. The message was pretty simple.

"Do you know a Neil Getzlow?" That was it. I don't know why, but I absolutely knew this random guy was somehow tied to my hidden life. Suddenly, I felt compelled to take off my mask and expose the addiction and lies that I hid behind.

I told Amy that for the past five years I was actively looking at porn a significant amount of time—several times during the day, every day. And then I dropped the atomic bomb— over those five years I had met more than a dozen women online and paid them to meet up in person and have sex with me. Finally, the mask was gone. Admitting everything that I did, fully and completely, was the first step in attempting to break free from the sin that defined my life.

It turned out the guy messaging Amy was the ex-boyfriend of a girl I had seen for more than two years. He sent Amy images of the text messages I had sent and receipts of the money I had sent her. He then started to ask Amy if she wanted to get revenge on me with him. He sent an explicit photo of himself to Amy. How could I have let this happen? How could I have invited this evil into my house, my marriage, my family?

Are you ready for the miracle? I know I am about this time. Let's get to the good news.

After I shared the details of the addiction I'd been dealing with for decades with Amy, I feared the worst. She had every right to walk out on me. I deserved it. I was absolutely, 100 percent dead in my sin. But she looked me straight in the eyes and said, "How can I not forgive you? Jesus forgave me for my sins. I forgive you, Neil." That was my "God shot." I started crying. Amy started crying. Amy's grace and forgiveness were transformative for me in ways that I simply didn't understand at the time.

It was April 14th, six weeks since my trip to Chicago. That was the day I turned my life over to Jesus. Just a few days later, as I contemplated the changes that would need to take place in my life to follow him, I was overcome with fear, anxiety, and self-doubt. There was a pain in my stomach that was radiating throughout my entire body. As I laid in bed next to Amy, I couldn't move and could barely speak. When Amy asked me what was wrong, I told her it felt like there was a battle happening over my soul right then. She smiled and agreed, "Yes, there is. The devil knows he is losing you to God. He's doing whatever he can to keep his hands on you." Right as that last word left her lips, all that fear, anxiety and self-doubt just evaporated. Gone.

For the wages of sin is death, but the free gift of God is eternal life in Christ Jesus our Lord (Romans 6:23 NLT).

Nobody ever signs up to tell a story like this. Quite the opposite, actually. I think a lot of people addicted to porn, sex, drugs, and booze do what I did, spending years of energy trying to stuff my sins deep inside me so they would never get out. My mask was on so tight that I didn't take it off for anyone. There was nobody in my world that knew what was behind my mask. *Nobody.* I was alone and ensnared in my own sin. Fortunately, God had other plans for me.

I wish I didn't have to write a book that starts with me sharing the worst parts of my sinful life, trapped in the depths of hell, but here we are. Without chapter 1 of this book, there would be no subsequent chapters of my redemption. There would be no good news to share, at least not from my lips. I really don't have choice but to share this testimony. If a fifty-year-old atheist can find hope and salvation in God during the middle of a pandemic, it can happen for you too.

There's only one way to describe what happened to me. It was a miracle; I have no other answers.

There's no explanation how a middle-aged Jewish man by birth, atheist by faith, spiritually blind and trapped in the darkness of his own sin, now believes Jesus is the Messiah, right?

There is no other way to explain the transformation that took place in me and the new heart that I have.

There's no way to understand how I can go from never reading the Bible (and having no interest in it) to reading and listening to every word of it in about six months.

There's no way I could go from being trapped by addictions to running away from them at full speed.

There is no way I could go from spending Sundays watching the NFL to spending Sundays watching online sermons.

There's no way I could go from hating church to looking forward to it.

There's no other way to explain how a marriage on the brink of collapse has transformed into a marriage that is stronger than ever.

There's no way to explain that I am a man who has gone from letting shame feed my depression and anxiety to knowing exactly what my plan is every single day. Well, mostly. I'm still working on that one.

The only explanation for all of this is a miracle—the miracle of God's saving grace, mercy and forgiveness.

It's appropriate that my story of redemption happens in 2020, the year of Coronavirus. During a time when the whole world was putting on a mask to save lives, I was taking mine off to save my own life.

One year after my unmaking, my old life is gone. God absolutely helped me walk away from it. I picked up my cross and followed Jesus. God helped me cancel my *own* sinful culture and replaced it with one that is full of the Holy Spirit. I read and listened the *entire* Bible. I started going to church. I saved my marriage. I stopped drinking, stopped smoking pot. I lost thirty pounds and ran a half-marathon. Most importantly, I stopped using porn and everything that went along with that, and I haven't looked back. I know that sounds hard to believe. And frankly, it still amazes me.

I understand that for a lot of people, turning away from your sins is a constant struggle. For me, turning my life over to God and using His power to overcome my sin and addiction was easy. The hard part was still ahead—trying to convince Amy the man behind the mask was truly saved.

REFLECTION: THINK ABOUT THE THINGS YOU NEED TO UNMASK IN YOUR LIFE.

1] Does your partner feel you are open and honest in sharing what's going on in your world?

2] What are you doing to help build trust in your relationship?

3] Are you hiding anything from your partner that you need to unmask?

4] Are you being open and honest with God about your sins?

If you are still trapped by your sins, I encourage you to use this prayer as a starting point for help:

Father, I am so grateful and blessed that you are waiting for me in heaven with open arms. I know that I am a sinner, and I am living a life trapped by sin. I ask for Your forgiveness. I repent of my sins and turn my life over to Jesus Christ, my Lord and Savior. Work Your will through me Lord. Help me walk away from my sinful life, pick up my cross, and follow Jesus.

▪ CHAPTER 2 ▪

SHINING LIGHT ON THE DARK PLACES OF YOUR LIFE

When Jesus spoke again to the people, he said, "I am the light of the world. Whoever follows me will never walk in darkness, but will have the light of life."

—John 8:12 NIV

One thing COVID-19 forced me to do was find something besides sports to watch on television. As you will read later in my story, that was another destructive addiction for me. Maybe not as destructive as pornography, but it certainly played a large role in the damage I was inflicting on my marriage. Amy would be upstairs watching TV in bed while I would be downstairs watching whatever sporting event was on. It was not the best way to build a healthy relationship with your wife.

However, without sports to distract me, Amy and I discovered we could actually find things to watch together. One night, while surfing the interesting world of YouTube, we landed on *Good Mythical Morning*. This YouTube show (fifteen-minute daily episodes) had been on for nine years before I watched my first episode. They just completed their 1900th episode and have more than five billion views from fifteen million subscribers on YouTube. The hosts are Rhett and Link, two funny, likable guys talking about random oddities in the world, and doing random food challenges and other stunts. It's one of the most popular shows on YouTube. They might be the biggest TV stars you have never heard of.

The more I watched, the more I wanted to know about these two—they were that engaging. They were best friends since childhood and it's obvious by the connection and fun they have on set. I also discovered that they were followers of Jesus. Alright! I knew there was a reason God helped me find them.

Then shortly after I found them, I discovered they had hours and hours of discussion about how they "deconstructed" their faith back in 2019. While other Christ-followers were angry for their public deconstruction, it simply made me sad. This term is used to describe a process where people pick apart the basis of their Christian beliefs point-by-point, dismantling the foundations of their faith. Here I am, with all the joy and innocence as a new follower of Jesus, and the guys decided to walk away from a lifetime of belief. If these two could walk away, how easy is it going to be for me to give up down the road?

As I read more about Rhett and Link's stories, I found more and more deconstruction narratives popping up online. Surprisingly, these stories didn't make me question my newfound faith. In the past, I might have let the views of others influence my decisions and values, often leading to sinful consequences. Now, the only view that matters about my life is what God has to say. All these deconstruction stories didn't make it easier for me to run away. It made me think more about the importance of my own "construction" story and the need to share it.

When I first started my journey, I still found it hard to believe that God could care about a nobody like me. As I started shining a light on the dark places of my life, all I found was a weak and broken soul. And now not only was God going to forgive me for my sins but also use me to tell my redemption story with others? Why me? I'm nobody. Like I said, I had not read one page of the Bible until I was almost fifty years old. I had no faith to construct or deconstruct because I simply had no faith. Why did God pick me and compel me to share my construction story? It's because I now carry a light that must be shared with others to expose the darkness.

> *Paul says those who carry Christ carry a light in them that God shined into their hearts. And that light lives in fragile vessels—human bodies. On the other hand, you can't kill light. You can't gather up a bunch of darkness and bring it into the room with light and even do so much as dim a match with it. Light is always more powerful. So while lots can happen to mess up the vessel, the light will remain unscathed. And in fact, every chip and every crack is just another way for the light to spread. And while Paul and his traveling companions are being physically tortured, the light is spilling out all around them—to prisoners and jail guards and governors and Jews and Gentiles. He can't help but speak what he believes. And if it ends up being the death of them, it will be for the life of others (© 2019 Tara-Leigh Cobble, D-Group & The Bible Recap, Day 338, 2 Corinthians 1–4).*

What happened to me and the steps I took to rebuild my life were more like an emergency road repair project versus building a high-rise building. I was not just broken—my heart was smashed into thousands of pieces that I could never put back together again on my own. Whatever you want to call it, this book contains key pieces of the blueprint I used to replace and construct my new heart, defeat my sin, and rebuild my marriage.

I know at times Amy wonders about my commitment to her. Why didn't I just leave if I was unhappy and so eager to meet other women? What I quickly realized as I started to expose more and more light to my dark world was that my acting out wasn't a reflection of how I felt about Amy. Even though I was constantly sinning in an immoral way, my answer remained consistent—I still loved Amy and wanted to be married to her. The issues with shame, porn, sexual addiction, lack of identity, and lack of purpose were hidden and masked by the feelings of love I felt when Amy and I started dating.

As I look back now, all those feelings and sins I thought I had broken away from came roaring back the moment Amy told me she found Jesus just a few months after getting married. It filled me up with hate, not for Amy, but for Jesus. As a Jew (even a nonreligious, "only in it for the food and jokes" Jew), there was nothing that would make me squirm more than having to deal with Jesus and his followers. And now I was married to one? I did not sign up for this. That's not the life I wanted. At the time, I loved my sins more than Amy, more than myself, more than God. I was exactly the kind of sinner Jesus was talking about in John.

> *And this is the judgment: the light has come into the world, and people loved the darkness rather than the light because their works were evil. For everyone who does wicked things hates the light and does not come to the light, lest his works should be exposed (John 3:19–20 ESV).*

So, I tightened up my mask, stuffed all that hate and anger deep down, and embraced the nightfall. It was my way of ensuring that I never would have a relationship with Jesus. I glorified the darkness and worshiped every sin that man created in this world. That's where my construction story starts—with a heart full of something other than love for Jesus. Not a great way to start a relationship. How do you build upon that?

One of my favorite things to do is listen to sermons from a wide range of pastors on my daily run. One pastor who I have come to enjoy is John MacArthur from Grace to You Church in California. He shared something startling in a sermon that I couldn't get out of my mind during my entire run: *out of 1,189 chapters in the Bible, all but four include sin—the first two chapters of Genesis and the last two chapters of Revelations.*

In some ways, that filled me with comfort. The Bible is full of redemption stories. Sinner after sinner rises to extraordinary heights, gets drunk on pride, falls in some tragic way, and yet still has a chance for salvation thanks to the mercy and forgiveness of God.

◇◇

Friend, you've just unmasked your life to your significant other. Now what? Not surprisingly, I did not have the answer, at least initially. I had just outed myself about the double-life I was living, effectively killing both. Plus, at the time, Amy and I were locked down together due to the newly announced pandemic. There was nowhere for me to run. I needed the grace of God to pick up the broken pieces of my life and put me back together. Fortunately, Amy's faith wasn't wavering at all. She knew exactly what I needed, what we both needed.

When I first exposed my sinful ways to Amy, she went looking for support and advice in the only place she knew she could—The Rock of KC Church which had become her family over the past eight years. Pastor Curt Vignery and his wife, Brook, are sort of the marriage gurus of the congregation. Having gone through their own struggles and coming out with a stronger relationship, they conduct couples' sessions at the church and host weekly Facebook Live chats with practical marriage advice. These were the first people Amy called. Of course, Curt was more than willing to speak with me and hear my story. I set up time to meet with him at Laz Fit, the fitness gym he owns.

This first meeting with Curt was just a few weeks after my encounter in Chicago. If I described the person who surprised me in that Chicago hotel room as an offensive lineman, Curt was cut from the cloth of a chiseled linebacker. Actually, a better comparison might be Samson; a towering presence full of muscle. But he was a gentle giant. He displayed a genuine interest in learning about me and wanting to help.

That first conversation with him lasted about an hour. Remember, this is before I fully pulled my mask off for Amy, so I didn't expose all my darkness to Curt either. He gave me a few things to do right away: pray, be open and honest with Amy, and he suggested a book to read. Obviously, I initially ignored all of that advice. I was still in love with the darkness of this world.

Once I fully shined light on all my dark places with Amy, I set up another meeting with Curt. Before I went back to see him, I started reading the book he recommended, The *Last Arrow: Save Nothing for the Next Life* by Los Angeles pastor Erwin Raphael McManus. The book's premise is simple and comes from the story of Elisha and the king of Israel, Joash.

> *And he said, "Take the arrows," and he took them. And he said to the king of Israel, "Strike the ground with them." And he struck three times and stopped. Then the man of God was angry with him and said, "You should have struck five or six times; then you would have struck down Syria until you had made an end of it, but now you will strike down Syria only three times (2 Kings 13:18–19 ESV).*

We all begin this life with a quiver full of arrows. So, what are we going to do? Are we going to hold on to those arrows when they do no good going unused? Or are we going to keep firing arrows until you have nothing left to give? This was the first "religious" book I read when I started my journey (I actually listened to it as an audiobook when running), even before starting to read the Bible. I did not totally understand all the lessons it was trying to tell me. It felt like a self-help book more than anything. It wasn't overly preachy, and it fueled my curiosity about God—a curiosity that shows no sign of slowing down.

Curt's message to me during the second visit didn't change: pray, be honest with Amy, listen to her with a repentant heart, and keep reading and filling your soul up with the Word of God.

◇◇◇◇◇◇◇◇◇◇◇◇◇◇◇◇◇◇◇◇◇◇◇◇◇◇◇◇◇◇◇◇◇◇◇◇◇◇◇

Those first two conversations with Curt were brief and simple, and they were also the most important conversations I had in my journey, outside of those with Amy. Sometimes you need a coach in life to challenge you and share the hard truths that eventually lead you down the right path. Curt could absolutely pass as a football coach. In this case, he was my initial guide to go from the darkness to the light.

Ten months later, I reached out to Curt again to share my progress with him. Even though I didn't realize it at the time, those initial meetings with him were the catalyst to helping me find my purpose and identity in life. If you are struggling with porn or other addictions, find yourself someone to help you get started on your walk to freedom.

"Men can be paralyzed in addiction and sometimes we need help to get moving. It's important to have someone willing to get you moving in the right direction. Once you are moving and have momentum, it just keeps building," Curt told me. "You have to find someone to help you redirect your life. You have to live with a purpose. When you know your purpose, you live with freedom. A lot of people lean on religion not because they believe in Jesus but because it makes them feel better—it's a crutch. But it's not easy to follow Jesus. Most people don't want to pick up that cross, so they self-medicate on all sort of things. If we truly believe that God is our Creator, then everything flows through that and from that, and it centers you."

As I look back on my journey over the past year, finding my new identity freed me from the chains of sin that dominated my world every single day. I no longer defined myself by the title on my business card, the amount of money in my bank account, how big my flat screen TV was, or how many shots I could do without getting sick. I am a child of God. That's my identity, and that's given me the purpose and light I need to expose my dark places.

We also talked more about Erwin McManus and his books. Curt eventually labeled me in his phone as "Neil - The Last Arrow." I like it. I'm not going to stop striking the ground in living a life that glorifies God. I can't explain it. I just know that's my purpose moving forward.

"This book (*The Last Arrow*) encapsulated a lot of things for me. Even though I have accomplished a lot, I still felt I wasn't doing what God had made me to do," shared Curt. "It was linked to an identity that I had of myself that I don't like failure. But God created me *on* purpose *for* purpose, so I better get moving. What's the worst thing that could happen? It moved me from fear to faith."

"For whoever would save his life will lose it, but whoever loses his life for my sake will save it. For what does it profit a man if he gains the whole world and loses or forfeits himself?" (Luke 9:24–25 ESV).

"What's the worst thing that could happen?" Those words Curt shared with me are like what Amy told me at the beginning of this journey. "What do you have to lose? If you are right and there's no God, no heaven, no hell, well you haven't lost anything. But what if I am right? You've gained everything." I love those words, and they really set the tone for how Amy and I set out to rebuild our relationship. We've got nothing to lose and everything to gain.

Taking off my mask and exposing the dark places of my life for Amy didn't just burn down our marriage like a cigarette slowly smoldering. No. I took a barrel of gasoline, poured it on our relationship, and used a weapons-grade flame thrower to ignite it. Whatever our marriage was before I asked God for help was completely and totally gone. It wasn't easy, and it created a lot of pain and heartache, but that's what had to be done. Step one to rebuilding trust was being open and completely honest. I had to expose all my darkness and admit all of my sin. I followed Curt's advice and came to Amy with a repentant heart. There's no chance for trust to grow back without that.

What we also discovered is that we literally had to start our relationship over with God in the middle. I think Amy and I both realized that we had grown apart over the past six or seven years of our marriage. Most, if not all of it, was caused by the mask I had covering my life. I never let Amy in—I couldn't. I didn't want to give up the world I had created for myself.

I spent so much energy keeping those dark places hidden that I had no time or energy for anything or anyone else. I was constantly distracted trying to keep all the stories straight in my head about what I did during the day which fueled a constant sense of anxiety and stress. It was impossible for anyone to see that pain with my mask on. But underneath it all, I was obsessed with trying to justify my sinful lifestyle. That made having a deep conversation with Amy (or my kids, my family, my friends) nearly impossible. Ripping off my mask gave my mind more time to focus on rebuilding those critical relationships in my life—especially the one with God.

What did starting over look like?

First, we made a commitment to put God at the center of our marriage. Going to church every week, praying together, reading the Bible together, filling up on God throughout the work week. That's a non-negotiable for any couple looking to rebuild.

It meant being completely and totally honest when Amy wanted to know the details of my addictions. *Every detail.* She wanted to know about my porn habits, who the people were I met, how I found them, even what I thought when I was with them. It was certainly uncomfortable to answer those questions repeatedly. And there were times where I got frustrated with the constant doubting because I felt like she would never be able to see the new heart inside of me. But she eventually did. It didn't stop the questions, but it gave each of us an opportunity to show our vulnerability, something we had never done before.

I used to take my phone with me whenever I would go take a shower. I used the excuse that I needed to charge it, but I really was just scared that an incriminating notification might pop up. Now, I turn over my electronics whenever Amy wants to see what I've been doing. She has the passwords and unfettered access to my phone and my laptop. We've installed location-sharing apps on both of our phones. It's a level of accountability I should have asked for much earlier in our marriage.

We bought two giant boxes of "conversation starter" cards for couples to fuel our initial discussions. We sat on our back patio for hours reading questions, listening, and learning.

Looking at porn on a consistent basis does desensitize you. It led to an unhealthy view of sex and clearly had a negative impact on our bedroom activities. I say this with a tone of disdain in my head. This common-sense knowledge about sex and marriage should be obvious, right? But that's what happens when darkness takes over; you lose any sense of what is right and what is wrong. That means we had to rediscover our sexual relationship as well. Having a connection *outside* the bedroom absolutely helps you have a connection *inside* the bedroom. All those soul-searching conversations we've had over the past year have absolutely helped turbo-charge our intimacy.

Curt had a great take on the importance of exposing your darkness to your partner. He said, "Your relationships can be better on the other side of pain. It can make space for a deeper level of love and intimacy. You might think they can never trust you again, but they can and will. It doesn't happen overnight, and there is a process, but it does appear. Just keep striking the ground."

REFLECTION: THINK ABOUT THE DARK PLACES OF YOUR LIFE THAT YOU NEED TO EXPOSE TO LIGHT.

1) What sins in your life do you need to expose?

2) Is there something holding you back from having God at the center of your life?

3) Do you feel you have a defined your purpose and identity in life? If not, how can you reconstruct your relationship with God?

CHAPTER 3

SHATTERED LIFE – SEDUCTION OF MY CULTURE

Now the serpent was more crafty than any beast of the field which the Lord God had made. And he said to the woman, "Indeed, has God said, 'You shall not eat from [a]any tree of the garden'?" The woman said to the serpent, "From the fruit of the trees of the garden we may eat; but from the fruit of the tree which is in the middle of the garden, God has said, 'You shall not eat from it or touch it, or you will die.'" The serpent said to the woman, "You surely will not die! For God knows that in the day you eat from it your eyes will be opened, and you will be like God, knowing good and evil." When the woman saw that the tree was good for food, and that it was a delight to the eyes, and that the tree was desirable to make one wise, she took from its fruit and ate; and she gave also to her husband with her, and he ate. Then the eyes of both of them were opened, and they knew that they were naked; and they sewed fig leaves together and made themselves loin coverings

—Genesis 3:1–7 NAS

Most days the old life I left behind in 2020 seems a million light-years away, but there are moments where I'm reminded that my past isn't that far away. While I might be saved by God's grace and mercy, it doesn't mean my actions are not still reverberating around the universe.

One such moment occurred during the summer of 2020 while attending our weekly church service. At this time, the church brought in Laila Mickelwait as a guest speaker. Don't know who Laila is? I didn't either, but we all should.

Laila fights sexual abuse and trafficking as part of Exodus Cry and founder of Traffickinghub.com (https://traffickinghub.com). Through the work of her organizations, she has gone toe-to-toe with the corporation behind PornHub.com. Their efforts led to a December 2020 *New York Times* article exposing how PornHub has become a dangerous repository for videos of underage sex, rape, and sex trafficking. The article, combined with Laila's efforts, have forced PornHub to make changes to their platform making it harder to post illegal content—an important first step in slowing down the influence of porn in our culture.

The more stories Laila and her organizations shared about the rape and trafficking videos being posted online and the victims behind those videos, the more uncomfortable I felt. I can't tell you how many videos I watched on Pornhub. I don't think I watched anything that involved an underage girl, but how could I know for sure? None of the videos that I saw seemed to show anyone that was coerced, but did I know that for a fact?

Then I started thinking about all the women I met online. I didn't really know much about them at all. Was there a boyfriend or a pimp forcing them into this lifestyle? Were they in such dire financial circumstances that they saw no way out but through what was essentially prostitution? I will never fully know how my actions contributed to the pain of others, but it is something I will always regret. That's why I had to unmask my own struggles with pornography for the world to see—to bring glory to the power of God's forgiveness and to provide hope to others dealing with the same demons that I had to conquer. There is a way out. It's not too late to take back control of your life.

For my entire life, pornography seduced me away from my friends, my kids, and my wife. Porn was a gateway drug that eventually led to my abuse of sex. It ruined one marriage and nearly took down a second one. Unfortunately, I am not alone in the struggle. You likely have already heard these statistics, but the numbers on the porn epidemic across America are staggering. The following figures are from Covenant Eyes, an accountability app that helps people overcome their porn addictions.

- 28,258 internet users are watching pornography every second.
- $3,075.64 is spent on porn every second on the Internet.
- 90% of teens and 96% of young adults are either encouraging, accepting, or neutral when they talk about porn with their friends.

- 64% of Christian men and 15% of Christian women say they watch porn at least once a month.

- The first exposure to pornography among males occurs at twelve years old, on average.

Those numbers are like a gut punch to me as I read them. I was part of that culture. But that last number is truly heartbreaking. I was usually an underachiever in life, but sadly that's the one area I outpaced my friends. I was nine years old when I first discovered the "Playboy Forest."

That's where the seduction of my culture started—a wooded area behind my elementary school. The older boys called it the "Playboy Forest." It sounded more majestic at the time than it really was, but the allure of looking at naked images of women, even at nine years old, set me down the dark path of pornography. Who knew that this would what started to feed my addiction? I'm not sure why this had such a large impact on my life.

I only visited this area a handful of times, usually after school. I would ride my Huffy dirt bike to the entrance of the forest and wait for a few classmates to get there before we ventured in. We only had to take ten-to-fifteen steps down the dirt trail and through the trees to come to a little clearing. There was enough space to have four tree logs set up in a square for people to sit on. If you weren't looking close enough, you might think that we were sitting around looking at a pile of trash.

But upon further inspection, there was a stack of ripped up pages taken from various Playboy magazines. Now remember, this was long before the rise of the internet. Looking at crumbled up centerfolds was more than enough for us. We'd spend about ten-to-fifteen minutes rummaging through the pictures and then ride our bikes back home. It's a scene I can play back vividly in my mind even though it was forty years ago.

I used to think, *What's the harm in looking at pictures from a magazine?* For some people, maybe they feel there is nothing wrong. I know I felt that way for most of my life until I finally realized the harm that is causes. But at nine years old, nobody really tells you, "Hey, don't look at Playboy magazines. They objectify and harm women and can lead to other addictive behaviors." Well, at least I didn't have anyone tell me that.

As I said, this was just the start for me in forming a relationship with porn. After my parents divorced, we moved away from the "Forest" when I was eleven. I spent a lot of time as a latch-key kid alone in my mom's apartment. She would work during the day, leaving me ample time to go through her HUGE collection of Playboy and Penthouse magazines that would be sitting out in the open on her nightstands. (I'll get into more details on this piece of my childhood in the next chapter). The other benefit of moving into an apartment was getting access to cable television.

If you grew up in the 1980's with the early version of cable, you know one of the thrills was staying up late on the weekends while looking at the scrambled signal of a premium movie channel. Every five minutes or so, the signal would magically unscramble, and if the timing was right, you had a three-or four-second view of soft-core porn, depending on the movie playing.

As technology advanced, along came on-demand cable TV about the time I was fourteen years old. Now, this isn't the on-demand cable you are familiar with today. When it first arrived at my mom's apartment, on-demand was similar to what you might still find in a hotel room today - a scrolling list of movies you could purchase. Of course, I managed to find the pornography section and was tempted to hit the purchase button on the remote.

One day, I took a chance and hit it. The cable company was very nice to alert me that I could watch two minutes of a movie before I would get charged. So, I managed to watch that entire movie in two-minute chunks of time. I would watch for about a minute, cancel my purchase, and then purchase it again. I did that with several movies over the course of a month.

Then the cable bill came. You see, you couldn't really jump in and out of those movies two minutes at a time. Once you jumped in and then out, you were done. The next time you started the same movie, you were getting charged. So that $800 cable bill was not one of my finest moments. Of course, like any sinner, I denied I had anything to do with the list of obscene titles—yes, all the movie names were printed—that showed up on the bill. My mom managed to convince the cable company that it was a technical glitch that caused these movies to show up. Fortunately for my teenage brain, the cable company also deactivated the on-demand function on our cable box.

As if I didn't have enough images of sex poured into my soul, it was around this same time that my mom started having an affair with a married man, Bill. He would come over every Friday night, which was supposed to be his bowling night. They would sit at the dining room table, have a drink, and head down the hall to my mom's bedroom. Let me just say that the walls of my mom's apartment were not soundproof *at all.*

My culture wasn't just seduced, it was absolutely shattered into pieces by the nonstop assault of sexual pictures, thoughts, and sounds that I was exposed to as a teenager. I had no idea what a healthy sexual relationship looked like. I never considered the amount of harm pornography can produce in the lives of those who make and consume the product. Isolation and loneliness are, without question, the easiest ways for your enemies to exploit your worst sins. I carried that with me until I finally had to ask God for help to break free from those demons.

I can't imagine being a teenager and growing up in today's culture. Obviously, the rise of the internet and technology fueled the growth of porn online. Anyone with a decent mobile phone and camera can star in their own video and make money from it. Access is right there for everyone, and it goes beyond the easy access to porn. All you have to do is turn on the TV and there is a constant barrage of sexuality being paraded in front of you. On every channel, at all hours of the day, the media we consume drowns our souls in sex.

I have two sons from my first marriage and three stepsons. The oldest three are now in their twenties. The two youngest are both seventeen. I have failed all five as a father when it came to warning them about the dangers of pornography, because I never said anything about it as they were growing up. I think a lot of that stems from the fact that I didn't view myself as a credible source for them. They had no idea what was lurking behind my mask. But I knew.

How could I talk to my sons about porn, sex, and healthy relationships when I was trapped in a harmful addiction myself? I feared the words would just come out hollow. I tried to protect them in other ways, like by shielding them from inappropriate content on television or in the movies we would go see. But I threw in the towel when they were about fourteen or fifteen. There seemed to be no way to avoid being inundated with sexual images when leaving the house.

Amy and I caught one of her sons searching for pornography on the family iPad a few years ago. We tried to talk to him about it, but the message didn't seem to resonate. And again, I failed to address the issue like I should have. I felt like a hypocrite trying to explain the impact of porn on life and relationships. I couldn't address it with my stepson because it would mean admitting that I needed to address it in my own life.

◇◇

As I shared in the opening chapter, I have not looked at porn since April of 2020. The urge simply left my heart once I turned my life over to Jesus. I know that might seem hard to imagine for both the believer and nonbeliever alike. All I can say is, "Glory to God for helping me turn away from my addiction." But there are days that I wonder, *How could Jesus forgive and save me?* If there was a top-twenty-five - ranking of the world's biggest sinners from 2015 to 2020, I feel like I would have cracked the top ten. But that's what Jesus does. He spends more time with the sinners than he does with the righteous.

> *And as he reclined at table in his house, many tax collectors and sinners were reclining with Jesus and his disciples, for there were many who followed him. And the scribes of the Pharisees, when they saw that he was eating with sinners and tax collectors, said to his disciples, "Why does he eat with tax collectors and sinners?" And when Jesus heard it, he said to them, "Those who are well have no need of a physician, but those who are sick. I came not to call the righteous, but sinners" (Mark 2:15–17 ESV).*

If Jesus called me away from a life of sexual deviance and sin, I have no choice but to pick up my own cross, turn away from sins, and follow him. I do realize that for many other men, and a growing number of women, it's a daily struggle to resist the temptation of porn and sex in our world. Looking back on my own struggles, I wish I had done things differently to protect my mind and spirit and to avoid the seduction of my culture:

- First and foremost, I wish I had asked God for help earlier in my life. That's the first and most important step you can make if you want to unmask the evil in your life.

- I wish I had built a relationship based on trust with Amy from the beginning. I spent years hiding behind a mask to keep Amy from seeing the real me.

- I wish I had different conversations with my kids about sex and porn growing up. Hopefully, sharing this book with them will help in the conversations they have with their kids down the road.

- I wish I had kept better track of my kids' online activities. There are so many apps you can download now to help you fully understand what your kids are doing online.

- And finally, I wish I had the courage to identify my addiction and take accountability for it earlier in life. The relationships I ruined, the time I wasted, and the money I squandered . . . the price I paid has been staggering. Admitting you have a harmful relationship with porn and sex is critical. As you will read in the next chapter, the shame of my lifelong addiction was overwhelming and kept me in a negative cycle that spiraled out of control. It's important to be honest with yourself and find someone you can talk with to help you change that cycle.

The good news is that it wasn't too late for me to change my world and get pornography out of my life. If you are struggling, or know someone who is, there is still hope. It is not too late to reclaim your life, your partner, your family, and your friends.

Just ask God for help.

REFLECTION: THINK ABOUT HOW THE OUTSIDE WORLD IS SEDUCING YOUR CULTURE.

1] Are there elements of culture you are participating in that you know lead you to temptation?

2] How do you deal with your temptations when you are isolated and alone?

3] How are you holding yourself accountable to keep you from indulging?

4] Do you believe pornography has negatively impacted your life (or your spouse's life)? Are you using prayer to ask for God's help?

▪ CHAPTER 4 ▪

SHAME

"No temptation has overtaken you that is not common to man. God is faithful, and he will not let you be tempted beyond your ability, but with the temptation he will also provide the way of escape, that you may be able to endure it."

—1 Corinthians 10:13 ESV

The last few years of my addiction always included the same set of events leading up to my encounters. I worked from home during the week, always alone. Amy was at work and the kids were at school or hiding out in their bedrooms. That offered my mind plenty of opportunities to get distracted throughout the day. And soon, those distractions fed into my addictions—and then into the shame I had carried most of my life.

It didn't matter if I was sexually aroused at the time or not; I trained my brain to need porn to satisfy my loneliness. I could never pinpoint what the trigger might be on any given day. It might have been a negative email from my boss or possibly a stressful phone call. Maybe there was nothing going on at work and I was simply lonely, bored, or feeling unloved. Whatever the trigger was, it would set of a shift in my brain and send it into another universe. I was on autopilot.

At times, I knew what I was doing was wrong, but I couldn't stop myself, always rationalizing my behaviors. It would start with casual scrolling through Twitter. There were plenty of real-life women willing to share their most intimate moments with the world, all with just a simple click of the computer mouse. That first image I would stumble on sent me down a rabbit-hole of online porn, clicking from one woman's Twitter profile to the next, from one website to another. I'd do that for about fifteen minutes and go back to work.

I wasn't satisfied. I needed to look at more. After a few rounds of that game, suddenly the images alone were not enough; I needed the real thing. I used a variety of different web sites to look for women willing to trade sex for cash. I had a list of some women I would regularly visit, but if those women didn't interest me that day, I could find someone new in just minutes. As soon as I set a time to meet up with someone, that's when the rush kicked in.

There was no way I could turn back—my mind wouldn't let me. I'd meet them usually at their apartment or a hotel. We exchanged a casual hello, made some small talk, and then took care of "business." The instant the event was finished, the adrenaline evaporated and was replaced by an overwhelming sense of shame that kicked in with a vengeance. Before I could even walk back to my car, my brain would cycle through a million thoughts like:

- What have I done?
- Why can't I stop doing this?
- Does anyone know about what I'm doing?
- I don't know how to control this.

I always made the promise with myself, *If I just make it home and Amy doesn't know, I will never do this again. Never.* Unfortunately, that shame cycle just kept repeating, with porn in the middle of it. Over and over and over again. I ultimately discovered it was a cycle that was rooted in not understanding love as a child.

> *For I am not ashamed of the gospel, for it is the power of God for salvation to everyone who believes, to the Jew first and also to the Greek (Romans 1:16 ESV).*

I spent several years trying to tackle my own issues of shame, depression, anxiety, and porn addiction. It wasn't until I asked God for help that I was finally freed from my sins, and I could tackle the source of my shame. That was step one—asking God for forgiveness. Step two was unmasking my sins with a faith-based counselor. That's right, men, while you might be carrying shame around, there is absolutely no shame in talking to a professional counselor (one rooted in God) to help you work through whatever might be weighing you down.

As I mentioned in chapter 2, it is so important to find people that you can trust and help you in your journey. Pastor Curt, who you met earlier in the book, gave me a list of a few counselors he recommended. The first one I looked up felt like he was using some combination of religion and new age medical sorcery. Pass. I need to get Curt to update his list.

The second name I called was Bryan Vignery. Bryan is a coach and counselor based in Olathe, Kansas. He and his wife, Stephanie, have a marriage ministry called The Intentional Marriage that provides resources to help couples build a Christ-centered marriage. He seemed pretty legitimate, so I set up some time to talk with him. Remember, we are doing this in the middle of a pandemic, so our sessions are only on Zoom. Imagine sharing the worst details and behaviors of your life with a stranger on a computer screen! It's not comfortable at all but taking off your mask is not going to be comfortable at any time.

When starting to delve into my childhood, Bryan asked, "What's one of the first things you had to learn to do on your own?"

This was really the first probing question he asked me during our initial conversation. It seemed innocent enough. But that one question set us down path of unmasking the root cause of my shame.

While it was a simple question, it took me a few minutes to figure out what my answer was. And then, the lightbulb came on.

"I had to learn to be alone," I told Bryan. From there, fifty years of shame, depression, and anxiety seemed to unravel by pulling on this one simple piece of thread.

I had an older brother and two older sisters—I was the "accident" of the family—with nine years between myself and my next oldest sister, Lisa. By the time I was nine years old, my siblings were ready to move out on their own. It was around that same time that my parents announced they were getting divorced. I don't have a lot of memories from my childhood, but I vividly remember when my Dad sat me down on my bed and said he was moving out. I didn't realize how much and how quickly it would impact my life.

Within a matter of a few months, we sold the house my siblings and I grew up in, my brother and sisters moved out on their own, and I moved with my mom into an apartment. I went from living literally right behind my elementary school with countless friends in neighborhood to having to ride the bus to school with a bunch of kids I did not know. That's when the loneliness kicked in. Sure, I made a lot of new friends, many of whom I still consider good friends to this day. But instead of walking home from school with the group of neighborhood kids, I was walking home alone from the bus stop to an apartment with no other kids in sight.

My mom worked during the day, so I was the prototypical "latchkey kid" of the 80's: came home after school, ate all the junk food, and figured out how to waste time. In the summer, instead of being home alone for just a couple of hours each day, I was left alone for about forty hours a week, Monday through Friday.

Bryan then asked, "And when you were alone what did you do?"

Well, I did anything I could to keep my mind off being alone. I was fortunate enough to own an Atari video game system, the premier gaming system of that time. It was also right around this time that cable TV launched. I spent my afternoons watching *The Brady Bunch* and *The Munsters* and playing *Missile Command* and *Space Invaders*. This was also the time that I fell in love with sports. I wanted to be a sportscaster growing up (I ended up going to journalism school to do just that later in life), so I would spend my days doing play-by-play of my *Strat-o-Matic* (tabletop fantasy sports games) baseball and football games. There were also plenty of day baseball games on during the summer, so I would turn down the volume of the television and provide my own soundtrack to the games, sometimes even taking my cassette recorder to capture my imitation of Jack Buck and Harry Carey.

My obsession with sports was only a part-time boredom-cure. Remember the "Playboy Forest?" Well, now I didn't need a forest anymore, I was living in a kingdom of porn. While the video games and cable TV were good timewasters, they still didn't replace the loneliness I felt.

If I wanted the attention of girls as a preteen, all I had to do was take a walk into my mom's bedroom. She had two nightstands, and each one contained stacks of *Playboy* and *Penthouse* magazines. At the time, some people really did read these publications for the articles. I was not really all that interested in the politics of Ronald Reagan back then; I was captivated by the naked flesh I could see on the pages of the magazines. I'd spend my days during the summer imagining sexual relationships with these women.

Then I discovered another drawer in my mom's room with more hardcore porn. When that wasn't enough, I found a stash of pornographic videos in a different drawer. This is where my shame cycle started. I'm not good enough to have people want to spend time with me.

I never had a strong bond with my parents. When my older siblings had moved out, they didn't really spend a lot of time with me. I had to reach out for approval, affection, and love as there were not a lot of "I love you's" being said in our house growing up. In the absence of that, I turned to the pages of those magazines to fill the void in my life, which led to obsessions, which in turn led to unhealthy relationships and a self-fulling prophecy: *See, I'm right—I'm not good enough to be loved, to be anything but alone.* And the cycle would repeat. That's what I thought love was when I was twelve and thirteen years old. I thought love equaled sex. This misperception would follow me through most of my teenage and adult relationships.

A lot of times for me, the feeling following sex was one of intense shame and guilt, like I was doing something wrong (and that was just with people I was in a relationship with). When I had one-night stands or paid someone for sex, sometimes the shame would be unbearable. Yet the cycle continued.

"There are two places that shame comes from," Bryan told me. "It's inherited and it's created. The inherited side is the set of circumstances we are born into. Often people are born into a family that thinks it's not good enough, and then you pile on your own created shame cycle."

This is sort of one of those "lightbulb" moments for me as I tried to figure out why this cycle had such a strong hold on me. I always joked with my gentile friends about living with Jewish guilt, though It is very real. That guilt just didn't start with me or my siblings. My mom was passing the shame down to us just as she learned it from her mom, my grandmother.

Like I said, there weren't very many "I love you's" passed around growing up, but there was a lot of yelling. My grandma yelled at my mom, and then my mom yelled at her kids. But it was more than that. There was always this feeling around my family (especially on my mom's side) that we simply were not good enough.

That's really how this whole cycle started—with my mom telling us that we were not good enough. She never came out and said those words directly, but what she would do is compare her life to that of her brother and his family. My Uncle was a successful businessman, made a great income, and had the nice house and car. My mom was struggling to make ends meet in various jobs, lived in an apartment, and drove a beat-up car. He had one daughter and one son, roughly the same age as me. Growing up and even through my adult years, my mom was always comparing her family with his.

"Neil, isn't it great that your cousin is getting Bar Mitzvahed." I never did, of course.

"Neil, isn't it great that your cousin graduated college in just four years and has started his own business?"

"Neil, isn't it great that your cousin has a lake house now that I am going to visit? You should see it. It's magnificent!"

My reply to this last one was, "Mom, do you want to come to Kansas City and visit your son and grandkids for a change?" Her response was, "Eh, I don't know. What's there to do in Kansas City, anyways?"

On top of listening to my mom rain praise down on my cousin (which he absolutely deserved, he's a good mensch), she couldn't bring herself to throw any praise my way. Even at forty-eight years old, I let that bother me and impact my life. I had started my own communications consulting practice after leaving my corporate gig in 2018. I was fortunate to start my business with a handful of clients. Business was booming until 2020. You plan for a lot of things, but you don't really plan for a pandemic. COVID-19 put a deep freeze on my cash flow. As I was relaying this news to my mom, instead of offering words of encouragement or saying how proud she was of me for taking a risk, she responded, "Well, maybe you should have thought this out a little more ahead of time before going out on your own." *Sigh.*

I'm not good enough for her attention/support/encouragement/love, I would say to myself. That's how the cycle would simply spin out of control, impacting every meaningful relationship I had in my adult life.

Bryan told me, "Guilt says I *did* something wrong. Shame says I *am* wrong." It wasn't Jewish guilt I was carrying on my shoulders all these years, it was Jewish shame.

◇◇

> *"When you've lost your way, you are at a very significant moment of decision. You will either point the finger or you will make a confession. That's the turning point." —Pastor Paul Tripp, The Paul Tripp Podcast*

As I go back and read what I wrote above about my mom, I realize you might get the impression that I am blaming my sins on her. That is not the case. She made mistakes like every parent does, but I absolutely forgive her and take every opportunity I can to remind her of that. I have my own mistakes to account for as a father.

Certainly, the things I experienced as a child carried with me throughout my adult life, but to blame everything on my upbringing wouldn't be fair. That's why I love that quote from Paul Tripp. When I had nowhere else to turn and I had lost my way in life, was I either going to keep blaming someone else for my trouble, or was I going to confess my sins? That was my turning-point. It was time to stop blaming others, start holding myself accountable, and ask God for forgiveness.

Once I was able to unlock this piece to the puzzle, I could work with Bryan on how to rebuild that positive identity of myself. Again, it starts with God. We are all broken in some way. Maybe your story isn't as extreme as mine, but we all sin. Despite this, God never turned his back on me, and He won't on you either. All these years I was trapped in my sin, He was there waiting with open arms for me to come home to Him, just like the parable Jesus told of the prodigal son in Luke 15:11–32. God gets ALL the glory for my redemption. And it was God working through Bryan that helped break my shame cycle, allowing me to stop seeing myself as the old sinful Neil and instead see the positive scripts in my life.

Bryan told me, "The most important thing to think about are some of the traumatic things that happened to you in life that got you stuck in your shame. It's not like we just wake up and think, *I am a failure*. We get stuck in it because we believe we have it proven to ourselves over-and-over. Spiritually, we finally realize that God created us for a purpose and that we have value versus just existing and feeling worthless. It takes going from "I am [negative word]" to "I am [positive word]" statements. It takes just a morsel of inherent worth coming from God to spin it positive."

Obviously, the impact of breaking my shame cycle has been incredible. My addiction to porn is gone. There is no more sexual deviance in my life and no desire to return to that way of living. My depression and anxiety are much more controllable: sometimes I can go weeks without those anxious feelings returning. Going from *I am not good enough* to *I am worthy* has helped me deal with stress in a much healthier way. Where I would turn to porn before in stressful situations, I now turn to God.

Thanks to Him, I was able to overcome my shame and sin. But the bigger question—could Amy overcome it? Yes, she forgave me and helped send me on this spiritual journey, but that doesn't mean there still wasn't a lot of pain and anguish to work through. Jesus gave me a new heart, but Amy kept seeing me as the old Neil. Would she ever be able to see the new me?

REFLECTION: THINK ABOUT THE THINGS THAT CAUSE YOU SHAME.

1] How do you fill yourself up if you are feeling ashamed or unworthy? Do those actions lead to obsessive or addictive behaviors?

2] What's the turning point in your life? Is there something you are pointing your finger at instead of confessing?

3] How can you look to God to break your own shame cycle?

▪ CHAPTER 5 ▪

UNCONDITIONAL LOVE AND THE POWER OF FORGIVENESS

"The Pharisee stood by himself and prayed this prayer: 'I thank you, God, that I am not like other people—cheaters, sinners, adulterers. I'm certainly not like that tax collector! I fast twice a week, and I give you a tenth of my income.' But the tax collector stood at a distance and dared not even lift his eyes to heaven as he prayed. Instead, he beat his chest in sorrow, saying, 'O God, be merciful to me, for I am a sinner.' I tell you, this sinner, not the Pharisee, returned home justified before God. For those who exalt themselves will be humbled, and those who humble themselves will be exalted."

—Luke 18:11-14 NLT

That power of forgiveness and unconditional love is life changing. For me, it goes back to that moment at the start of my story when God helped me unmask all my sin to Amy.

This is an awkward (and probably gross) analogy, but stick with me. Think about the last time you had to vomit. For me, I remember feeling my stomach starting to gurgle and tighten up. I was feeling awful and curled up on the cold floor of the bathroom, starting to grab on to the toilet. Soon, that feeling slowly started to make its way up my body and just sat there in my throat. I knew it was going to come out and there was nothing I could do to stop it. Finally, the moment arrived and I literally spilled my guts repeatedly into that murky toilet bowl. But then, suddenly, I felt so much better. I could stand up again without the room spinning. I was so relieved that the sickness was just violently forced out of my body. I felt instantly healed.

That is exactly how I felt when unmasking my evil side to Amy. God was working His will on me and through me, forcing me to confess my sin. I could feel the words collecting in the pit of my stomach. There was a brief moment before those words spilled out of my mouth that I said to myself, *There's no going back once you start talking. Life changes forever.* And with that, I let it all out. It wasn't just about confessing my sins though; the only way for me to be saved (and forgiven) was to be truly repentant of my actions. As Paul said in II Corinthians 7:10 (NIV), "Godly sorrow brings repentance that leads to salvation and leaves no regret, but worldly sorrow brings death." Was I going to live or die? God told me through the next words that came out of Amy's mouth.

"How can I not forgive you? Jesus forgave me for my sins. I forgive you, Neil."

I replay that moment in my mind every single day and what it did for my life and our marriage. The miracle of our story isn't just about how a middle-aged Jewish/atheist got saved, although that's a big miracle. The other side to our story is even more significant. Those words that Amy spoke to me weren't just her words. It was God's will working through her. Without miracle number one, miracle number two would have never occurred.

It reminds me of the parable of the unforgiving debtor that Jesus told his disciples in Matthew 18:22–35. A debtor owed the king $1 million but couldn't pay it. The king threatened to sell the debtor, his wife, and their children to pay off his debt. Instead, he begged for forgiveness, and the king granted it. But then moments later, the debtor tried to collect the money he was owed from a fellow servant. When the servant asked for more time to pay him, the man had him arrested. Here's what happened when the king found out:

> *"Then the king called in the man he had forgiven and said, 'You evil servant! I forgave you that tremendous debt because you pleaded with me. Shouldn't you have mercy on your fellow servant, just as I had mercy on you?' Then the angry king sent the man to prison to be tortured until he had paid his entire debt. That's what my heavenly Father will do to you if you refuse to forgive your brothers and sisters from your heart" (Matthew 18:32–35 NLT).*

Would you be so forgiving if someone in your life told you how they sinned against you? Even though God has shown us mercy and forgiven us for our sins, how often do we refuse to extend that mercy to someone else who we feel has wronged us? If the tables were turned, I'm not sure (at least before I was saved) I would have shown the same level of mercy that Amy did for me. I also think about what our life would look like if she didn't or couldn't forgive me. What if Amy acted more like the debtor instead of the king? Things would look exponentially different now. I'm assuming it would have led to the ultimate destruction of our marriage.

As Pastor Curt told me, Amy's forgiveness wasn't for me, it was for her. "The power of forgiveness is for you as a forgiver. If there wasn't forgiveness, she would always hold on to your sin. That leads to other sins and sickness. Lack of forgiveness is the root of bitterness. The power of forgiveness releases you to walk in freedom. If there's any hope of reconciliation, forgiveness creates the space for it. It creates the fertile ground for it to happen. If there is any hope in changing, you have to release whatever you are holding on to and forgive."

Amy's forgiveness (and the forgiveness Jesus offered both of us) was life altering, but that didn't mean it made our lives any easier initially. We literally had to clean up my vomit from the floor of our marriage and try to rebuild trust in our relationship—trust that was completely destroyed by my addictions.

Amy is always quick to remind me, and rightly so, that just because she forgives me doesn't mean there are no consequences for my actions. Over the past year, I've not only had to learn to walk in the new faith growing inside me, but I also had to learn how to be accountable for my past actions. It has meant letting go of control of my life, and giving that power to God

I must accept that He will work His will on us and through us; we don't have much say in that. I've also had to give up control in my marriage. When I say "control," I'm not talking about ruling over Amy's actions. I'm talking about the management of information. The elastic band that was holding my mask so close and so tight to my face for decades was made of information. If I was going to be in control of my sins and keep them hidden from the world, the less anyone knew about me the better.

Amy knew extraordinarily little about what I did when she wasn't around. I was vague about the details of my job. I was generic about how my evenings were hanging out with my friends. I shared little-to-no information about our finances. If she asked how I was doing, I was usually just "okay" and "fine." I kept all that information as close to me as I could. That was my way of staying in control, keeping that mask on tight. What seems ridiculously obvious to me now wasn't registering with me at the time—that's a horribly selfish way to treat anyone, especially your spouse. God commands men to honor their wives.

> *In the same way husbands should love their wives as their own bodies. He who loves his wife loves himself. For no one ever hated his own flesh, but nourishes and cherishes it, just as Christ does the church (Ephesians 5:28–29 ESV).*

So, if I was truly repentant and ready to follow God's wishes, I had to demonstrate that to Amy in my actions, not just my words. It started with sharing everything, even the most basic data points of my life. I started sharing my location through an app on my phone, sharing the passcodes to my laptop and phone, and handing over my electronics whenever she felt the urge to see what I had been doing. Most importantly, I started sharing with her what's on my mind and what's in my heart. The stone-heart God took out of me was replaced with one of flesh. As written in Ezekiel 36:26 (NIV), "I will give you a new heart and put a new spirit in you; I will remove from you your heart of stone and give you a heart of flesh."

That new heart beating in me is still not perfect, and it still struggles with sin every day. That means there are days where I revert to old behaviors of shutting down and shutting off information flow when something is bothering me instead of sharing it readily. But that heart continues to be shaped and molded by God. He is turning my life around, and He's turning my relationship with Amy into a blessing.

Over the past year, I've had to learn a lot about forgiveness. Part of breaking my shame cycle was learning to stop pointing the fingers at others for my sins. Even though my childhood exposure to pornography is something I carried around with me my entire life, I had to learn to forgive my mom and stop pointing to her as the trigger for my future actions.

For weeks after the Chicago couple shook me down for cash in their hotel room, I desperately wanted to call the police and report them. Why? I hated them for exposing my secrets. They were ripping the mask off that I had so carefully maintained for years. Today, I absolutely forgive them. In fact, if I were to see them walking down the street, I'd likely run up to them, shake their hands, and thank them for the role they played in turning my life around.

More importantly, I've also had to learn how to forgive myself. There are days that I wake up, think about my past, and shake my head in disgust. I am, without question, the biggest sinner in the world. How can anyone possibly forgive me for what I have done? How can I forgive myself for what I have done? But then I think about the words of Paul the Apostle.

> *I thank him who has given me strength, Christ Jesus our Lord, because he judged me faithful, appointing me to his service, though formerly I was a blasphemer, persecutor, and insolent opponent. But I received mercy because I had acted ignorantly in unbelief, and the grace of our Lord overflowed for me with the faith and love that are in Christ Jesus (1 Timothy 1:12–14 ESV).*

Here's one of the greatest followers of Christ expressing his astonishment at being picked to serve Jesus because he considered himself the chief sinner in the world at that time. And though he still finds sin in his heart, he is saved and justified by the grace of Jesus. It's a great reminder that we must continue to repent of our sins and submit to God. If Jesus can forgive me and my multitude of sins, I need to forgive myself as well. It's a work in progress, but it's getting easier to look myself in the mirror and not see a sinner but instead a child of God.

◇◇

> *"Do not be afraid; you will not be put to shame. Do not fear disgrace; you will not be humiliated. You will forget the shame of your youth and remember no more the reproach of your widowhood" (Isaiah 54:4 NIV).*

Time and time again since I unmasked my life, I've feared being shamed: afraid of feeling disgraced and being humiliated. But consistently, I have seen that fear is unfounded.

It was late summer in 2020 on a random Friday afternoon when my phone lights up with a number I don't recognize. I quickly hit the ignore button and let it go to voicemail. Sure enough, a few minutes later, the voicemail notification pops up. I always fear the worst when I get calls from random numbers, which should not be a surprise after reading the opening few paragraphs of chapter 1. But this message was actually just what I needed to hear.

"Hi Amy, this is Dane from Rock of Kansas City. We're just calling members of the church to check in on you during the pandemic and make sure your family is doing well. Call me back if you want to talk."

It wasn't the longest voicemail, and it wasn't even directed at me, but it sent a jolt of energy surging through me. That week, members of our church leadership were doing some mental health outreach to our community, checking in on families and making sure all was well during the pandemic.

I had been attending church every week with Amy for a few months, but we never had an opportunity to connect with people. Having someone from the church reach out and check in on us filled my heart with a love that I was not used to feeling. That one call solidified my confidence that I was indeed headed down the right path. I was so excited to get that message from Dane. I knew that forming a deeper relationship with fellow brothers and sisters in Christ was going to be critical to my journey, but I had no idea how to do it. God offered me a lifeline through Dane, and I quickly grabbed on.

I called him right back, told him I was Amy's husband, and that we were so thrilled to be part of The Rock of KC church family. The more we talked, the more compelled I felt to share the beginnings of my testimony. I didn't share every gory detail of how I got saved, but I certainly shared plenty about the demons I had battled for most of my life. Dane didn't seem bothered at all.

Later that summer, Dane invited Amy and me to join their weekly Connect Group with members of our church. Again, my old instincts started to flare up. I remember telling Amy how nervous I was to go to this group. I'm an introvert at heart, and the thought of going to hang out with people that I don't know and talk about the Bible seemed like a bad idea for a guy who is still in the infancy of his relationship with Jesus. Yet once again, there was no reason to be afraid.

The group welcomed Amy and me with open arms, and we quickly felt like part of their Connect Group family. Ultimately, I emailed an advanced copy of chapter 1 of this book to a few members of our group. I absolutely felt the fear of how others would react to the graphic details of my sinful past. As God told Isaiah in 54:4, there is no reason to be afraid. The response from those who read my spiritual journey was humbling.

I was not judged for my prior actions; there was just unconditional love and support from my church family.

The responses were, "We are all sinners—we all have our own battle scars. There is nothing to be ashamed of. We still love you." And what really blew me away was that I had people tell me, "Your story is so inspirational to our own faith. It's always so encouraging to see how God works His will through other people. Don't be ashamed by your story. Use it to glorify God."

This was another reminder about God's saving grace and mercy. No matter our sins, we are forgiven for our transgressions and are still very much loved. It's important that we surround ourselves with people that support us on our journey, know we are full of sin, and love us anyway. I'm so grateful to God for bringing those people into my life.

Exposing your sins to fellow believers is relatively easy. The harder part has been telling the people that love you and have been by your side for your entire life that you have been a horrible sinner. I was concerned with their reaction to my sinful life and my path to redemption. I was worried how they would react to my new relationship with Jesus. After all, we grew up Jewish and Jesus wasn't really a big topic in our house. Then again, neither was Moses. My siblings and I didn't have the tightest of relationships since they were out of the house before I was ten years old. All I can say now is I am blessed to call them family and appreciate the unconditional love they showed.

I told my sister Lisa first. When I was in St. Louis over the summer of 2020 to help take care of my Dad, I had an opportunity to sit down with her and tell her my story. Her reaction was what I expected—she was shocked. She wanted to make sure I was okay. She wanted to make sure Amy was okay. She was genuinely happy for me and my newfound faith, although she did say very nicely that it wasn't for her. Sharing my story with her also led as down the road to a deeper conversation about our parents and how our childhood impacted both our lives.

At the exact moment we finished our conversation, a commercial on television came on and asked the question, "Have you found Jesus?" We both looked at each other, slightly freaked out, and she asked if I planted that advertisement. "Uh, no. I didn't." What may have been a coincidence was just a reminder that I was on the right path and needed to share my journey with my other siblings.

Next, I sought out Dori and Gregg. We have more of a "texting" relationship than anything else. I wasn't about to text my story, so I decided to drop them a random email. I'm better with writing words than I am speaking because I tend to have more courage behind the keys of my laptop. Here's the email I sent to each one in January 2021.

> *Happy new year and all that stuff! Hope you had a good holiday season. So . . . I wanted to share something with you that I know is going to seem like it is coming out of left field—and honestly it really has come as a surprise to me. But I feel compelled to share my experience with you. Ever since COVID-19 sort of put life on hold, and with my 50th birthday happening, and Dad's illness and passing, I've been doing a lot of thinking and reading about life and what's ahead. And yes, that very much includes*

> *reading the Bible. I know we've never really talked about religion much. I do know that I love our Jewish culture and now I am learning to love the greatest Jew of them all—Jesus. Yes, that Jesus. (I'll give you a few minutes to pick yourself up off of the floor). I will always be a Jew. That will never change. I'm just adding a key piece to my life (Jesus) that has been missing in my world and has truly changed my heart. Now, there is one more piece to the puzzle that I have to share. It's the attached story. I'm writing a book about my experience over the past year. There are some very specific events that sort of brought all of this to a head over the past year. It's going to be pretty shocking to read but just know that I am in a good place—and Amy and I together are in a good place. I'm just at the beginning of this journey but I wanted to share.*

It probably took me ten minutes to work up the courage to hit SEND on the email to each of them. It took them both about a week to respond; that was a week of me wondering if I had sufficiently freaked them out and if they were trying to figure out how to answer me. I gave Gregg a little nudge and texted him about the latest baseball trade rumors. He called right back.

"Neil, I'm still processing what you sent me. I've read it twice, probably need to read it a few more times to understand what the heck happened. But you're my brother, what you do is your business, I'm not going to stop being your brother because you are out running around on Amy." Gregg definitely has a very dark sense of humor, so I could tell he was trying to take the awkwardness out of the conversation. He had also called my mom and told her I was going to become a rabbi, but fortunately she didn't believe him. That was the extent of our conversation on the topic of my sins, and we quickly moved to talking about sports and how crazy the world is today. I considered that a victory.

When Dori's return email hit my inbox, I was bracing for the worst. Instead, her email filled me with hope. Here's a portion of her response:

> *Someday when we both get time, I would like to talk to you about the religious part of your journey. My friend, Roy, was always pushing me to get saved and I would go with him sometimes. I have had conversations/disagreements with him and a few others when discussing religion, but they never saw things through my perspective of how all this G-d stuff works. In the Bible belt of the south all around me are the Baptists, and whenever I talk to friends etc., they always say pray to G-d and He will let you know what to do. I have never understood that, and I had a hard time understanding how everyone can believe as they do. In a way, I guess we were shortchanged in the religious department. Maybe I would think differently if we knew more about the Jewish religion and its beliefs. Anyway, maybe once COVID goes away and we can start visiting again, I would really like to sit down and talk with you.*

By the time I finished her email, the tears were rolling down my cheeks. I don't know where her journey will take her—maybe it won't even end in her getting saved—but I am looking forward to having that conversation with her. I am just absolutely humbled that God could work His will through a sinner like me to get one more person into His kingdom. All glory to God!

REFLECTION: THINK ABOUT LOVE, FORGIVENESS AND MERCY IN YOUR LIFE

1) Do you find it easy to forgive people, or do you hold on to your anger? Who are the people in your life you need to forgive?

2) When you seek out forgiveness from others, how do you ensure you have a repentant heart?

3) How can you use your own redemption story with God to encourage others?

■ CHAPTER 6 ■

WORSHIP OF THE HIGH PLACES

One of the teachers of the law came and heard them debating. Noticing that Jesus had given them a good answer, he asked him, "Of all the commandments, which is the most important? The most important one," answered Jesus, "is this: 'Hear, O Israel: The Lord our God, the Lord is one. Love the Lord your God with all your heart and with all your soul and with all your mind and with all your strength.' The second is this: 'Love your neighbor as yourself.' There is no commandment greater than these. Well said, teacher," the man replied. "You are right in saying that God is one and there is no other but him. To love him with all your heart, with all your understanding and with all your strength, and to love your neighbor as yourself is more important than all burnt offerings and sacrifices." When Jesus saw that he had answered wisely, he said to him, "You are not far from the kingdom of God." And from then on, no one dared ask him any more questions.

—Mark 12:28-34 (NIV)

June 14, 2019. I was standing outside The Blue Line hockey bar in downtown Kansas City. Several hundred other St. Louis Blues fans were with me clogging a city street watching TVs on the *outside* of the bar. The inside was filled to capacity. It was game seven of the Stanley Cup Finals between the Blues and Boston Bruins. A few days earlier, I had driven to St. Louis with my son, Max, to watch game six with my lifelong friend, Robert. I had paid $5,000 for three tickets to watch the Blues lose, but I didn't care. We were there to watch history. Never had our team been in position to win a championship.

Before the game, there was a nervous energy that was keeping everyone relatively quiet, but once the Blues led 2-0 after the first period, our nerves turned into two hours of celebrating, crying, and drinking . . . *a lot*. As the final seconds ticked off the clock, I hugged Max and then ran around looking to hug everyone else. Max and I took a victory lap through the bar while the Blues theme song for the season, "Gloria" by Laura Brannigan, was blaring from inside.. The St. Louis Blues were Stanley Cup champions. The team I lived and died with as kid, teenager, and adult finally won it all. As I was driving home, likely intoxicated, I thought to myself, *It just doesn't get any better than this.*

Well, I was wrong. About eight months later, I was at Tower Tavern with my wife, stepson, and my son (Max) watching the Kansas City Chiefs play the San Francisco 49ers in the Super Bowl. The last time the Chiefs had made it to the Super Bowl was 1969, so inevitably there was a ton of pent-up excitement in the city. In fact, I had to pay $120 to ensure I got a table inside the bar just to watch the game, but it came with unlimited chicken wings, so it was worth it.

The game wasn't decided until the fourth quarter, so there was plenty of drinking to help keep the nerves at bay. Once again, my favorite team was about to win a title. This time, as the final seconds of the game counted down, the owner of the bar handed out bottles of "Chiefs' champagne" to some patrons. I got one, and when the clock read *00:00,* I sprayed that bottle all over my section of the bar. The entire place was covered in a sticky, sweet mixture of champagne and beer.

I surveyed the damage and all I could see were the smiling faces of my friends. It was such a great feeling. I sent my wife and stepson home, then Max and I drove downtown to celebrate. The entire city migrated down there to do the same thing. We parked about a half-mile away from the Living Room in Power and Light District (the official gathering spot of the city) and started walking.

We traded high-fives with every single person we passed. The traffic was at a standstill and horns were blaring; the entire city was delirious. A few days later, the city gathered again for a Super Bowl parade. Patrick Mahomes' bus stopped right in front of us. Someone from the crowd tossed him a can of beer, he caught it, chugged it, and slammed the can to the ground. I turned to Max with my mouth wide open—It was like I had just witnessed the greatest thing I had ever seen in my life. And once again I thought to myself, *It just doesn't get any better than this.*

After the Super Bowl, I joked that I could retire as a sports fan since my teams had finally made it to the "promised land." Well, it seemed God took my joke literally when just a few weeks after the Super Bowl parade, the entire sports world was shut down by COVID-19.

We are commanded to love God *first*. Above everything else, love God with all your heart, soul, and mind—there's just nothing more important. Unfortunately, that really didn't describe my relationship with God for most of my life. In reality, for all my life up until 2020, I didn't have a relationship with God at all. I had a relationship with sports, and it was as deadly to me as my addiction to porn.

One of the first sermons I attended in person was about "removing your high places." As my pastor from the Rock of KC Church, Phillip, described it, high places were holy places in the Bible that people would go to and worship God. But some kings turned those high, holy places into locations of idolatry and sin.

He went on to describe a high place "as any place where we continually return to and dishonor and disobey God. I know it's wrong, I know God doesn't want me to do it, but I gain pleasure from it. That's a high place." For some people, it is sex; for others it is money; for other people, it is gossip. For me, there was no doubt that sports were my own man-made high places, my "except."

On our first date, Amy asked if I was into sports. I wasn't completely open and honest with my answer. If I was being truthful, I would have said, "Amy, I will love you *except* when the Jayhawks/Blues/Chiefs/Cardinals/some random international soccer games are on TV." When you allow your "except" and your high places to rule your life, you are leaving room for destruction by the enemy.

How could loving sports be a sin? The overwhelming majority of all the positive memories I've had are probably sport-related. From attending my sons' sporting activities to taking them to some of the biggest events in the sports world, sports and their superstars have brought me so much joy that's it hard to think that any of it could have been harming me in anyway. Let me make it clear: following, watching, attending, and rooting for your favorite teams is not a bad thing. It can be a healthy escape from the daily grind and offer a way to connect with family, friends, and your community. I still watch on television and still plan on going to games with my sons.

What I am saying is that you have to make sure your priorities are straight. Love God first. Be fanatical about worshiping God, not sports teams. That's where I short-circuited myself. I never believed in God, so I had nothing to fill up my mind and heart with but the passions of this world. For me, sports were my escape from reality as a kid when I was left home alone while my mom was at work. I remember coming home from school and turning on the TV to catch the last three innings of the Chicago Cubs game on WGN before flipping to WTBS to watch the start of the Atlanta Braves game. It goes back to the shame cycle I shared in chapter 4. Just like porn and sex, as I got older, I used sports to fill up my heart, medicating myself against the depression and anxiety that I was trapped in.

Sports were a gateway drug, of sorts, for me. Watching the game itself wasn't the issue—it's what would happen when I would watch the game.

- I would get ridiculously angry if a college kid missed a free throw at the end of a basketball game. I have broken more television remotes watching sports than I care to admit.

- I would get irrationally depressed when my team lost, or just as senselessly happy if they won. I remember a year that Kansas University got knocked out of the NCAA basketball tournament early when they were ranked number one in the country. I laid on the floor of my living room and cried, not moving for an hour after the game. Did I mention I was twenty-seven years old at the time and not seven? Not good. My daily moods were determined by how the previous night's game went.

- If I would meet up with friends to watch a game, I would go out for three-to-four hours at-a-time without Amy.

- During March Madness, I would be hanging out with friends every weekend of the entire month, leaving Amy and my family home alone.

- If we would go to a bar to watch the game, we would have shots, vodka tonics, and Long Island iced teas before, during, and after, regardless of how our team performed. One night I literally passed out drunk at our favorite sports bar during a basketball game and had to be helped out to my friend's car.

- During commercial breaks, once the alcohol kicked in, I would pull out my phone and scroll through Twitter, getting into worthless arguments about the game or sneaking a look at porn when nobody was looking.

- I drove home drunk on more than one occasion. For whatever reason, God made sure I didn't hurt myself or others while doing so, but there were times I truly had no idea how I managed to get myself home without getting arrested. A few times, my boys would see me stumbling in from the garage—a fine example I was setting for them.

- Of course, stress drinking watching a game made me stress eat, and therefore overeat.

- Then, for good measure after I got done eating, I would proceed to turn on SportsCenter to see what the national reporters were saying about *my* team before passing out on the couch.

It wasn't just sports and its heroes that I turned into idols. I did that with everything in our current culture: I idolized rock stars, movie stars, TV stars. Anyone in the spotlight, big or small, I used as a high place. You could replace sports with any Avengers movie, and it would involve the same sinful behaviors I listed above.

If any of that sounds familiar to you because it's part of your own lifestyle, I can tell you there is hope. You've got to tear down your high places, take off your mask, and love God first. It's as simple as that.

For those who live according to the flesh set their minds on the things of the flesh, but those who live according to the Spirit, the things of the Spirit. . . . For if you live according to the flesh you will die; but if by the Spirit you put to death the deeds of the body, you will live (Romans 8:5, 13 ESV).

I absolutely notice when I don't get enough God in my life. I feel like a house plant without water with leaves drooping and turning brown. But pour some water on me and I spring back to life. The perfect weekend for me doesn't revolve around sports anymore, and not because Amy and I are out on the town or have some magical experience walking around The Plaza shopping district in Kansas City. Sometimes we only leave the house on the weekend to go to church on Saturday night. It's a time of slowing down and enjoying each other by listening to the Bible, watching sermons online, and making dinner together, all with little noise from the outside world. It feels so good. I can tell that my soul craves that nourishment.

It is so easy to starve myself during the week with work and other distractions. So, when I can reconnect with God like that on the weekend, it just makes a huge difference. The more you fill up with the goodness of God, the more you want— and the easier it gets to walk away from those high places in your life causing you to sin and idolize. I'll be honest, I haven't completely walked away from sports. I never will. I still have more than a passing interest in the fates of my teams, although not nearly to the degree I used to. It just doesn't rule my world anymore. God does.

◇◇

Sometimes, that high place isn't a "high place" after all. It's God's hand.

On October 25, 1987, my brother, Gregg, and I attended my first real concert—U2. The Arena (yes, that was the name of the old barn) in St. Louis was sold out. There were 20,000 people packed into a building that would start to feel uncomfortably full with 17,000 in the stands. Up and down the aisles it was a sea of humanity. We were all there to worship at the altar of U2 and Bono, the lead singer. And for good measure, game seven of the 1987 World Series was also taking place that night between the St. Louis Cardinals and Minnesota Twins.

The building was pulsing with an electricity that I still can feel to this day when I recall the event. As a seventeen-year-old, St. Louis-born-and-raised teen, this was no doubt going to be the greatest night of my life, and the night didn't disappoint.

We somehow were able to buy tickets over the phone when they first went on sale months earlier. I would say that half of my high school class was likely at the show as well. Like most St. Louisans, my brother Gregg was a die-hard Cardinals fan too, so he managed to get in a portable four-inch TV so we could watch the game while attending the concert. There weren't smartphones at the time to help; it took real a TV with a real antenna picking up a real over-the-air signal to keep up with the score.

When it was time for U2 to start their set, Bono came charging out on stage in a Cardinals jacket singing "Where the Streets Have No Name." The crowd absolutely went nuts, and I could feel the concrete underneath my feet shake. It stayed that way for the next two hours as U2 ripped through its emotional catalogue of songs.

Without a doubt, it was the greatest concert I have ever seen in person, even to this day. Near the end of the show, I leaned over to my brother (who was in the row right in front of me) to see the Cardinals going down in defeat, but it really didn't matter that night. I was captivated by what I was witnessing. For the last song, U2 played "40," their traditional ending song. The last verse says, "How long to sing this song?" As U2 was exiting the stage one member at a time, the crowd was serenading them—something that happens at every show. It was the moment I was waiting for.

Hooooooowwwwww longgggggg to sing this songgggggg?

Hooooooowwwwww longgggggg to sing this songgggggg?

Hooooooowwwwww longgggggg to sing this songgggggg?

Unceasingly, 20,000 people sang these six words at the top of their lungs for a good five minutes after the show ended and U2 was long-gone. I joined in, and the tears were streaming down my face, feeling overwhelmed by the power of the moment. When the singing stopped and the lights finally came up, my brother and I were just sitting there, unable to move. Drained by the experience, Gregg turned around and said, "Neil, what you just saw will never be repeated. That was a once-in-a-lifetime experience." He was right.

Throughout my entire life, I filled my heart and mind up with music and sports, not God. I treated my favorite bands and sports heroes as idols—I worshiped them fully, and I lived and died by their success. They were my high places, so that night felt like a religious experience for me. It's how I defined religion my entire life, at least until COVID-19.

I just didn't know that God was there that night back in October of 1987.

Today, one of my favorite parts of the whole Bible is Psalm 40. Even though I had never read it before I was saved, when I finally did, the words felt so familiar to me.

> *I waited patiently for the Lord to help me, and he turned to me and heard my cry. He lifted me out of the pit of despair, out of the mud and the mire. He set my feet on solid ground and steadied me as I walked along. He has given me a new song to sing, a hymn of praise to our God. Many will see what he has done and be amazed. They will put their trust in the Lord (Psalm 40:1–3 NLT).*

The more I thought about those words, the more familiar they sounded. After thirty-three years, the lightbulb finally came on for me. In my mind, I flashed back to the lyrics to U2's "40", the song 20,000 people all sang at that concert back in 1987. I can still here Bono's voice echo in my head as he sang those exact words from Psalm 40.

Mind blown. Psalm 40 *was* U2's "40". Even though I didn't realize it at the time, God was with me in 1987 as a geeky teenager just as he was with me as a sinful adult. He was always faithful, always waiting for me to come home into His arms. I simply can't express how much joy it brings to my heart to realize that.

Four months before his ninetieth birthday, my dad died on July 24, 2020 after a long, slow battle with cancer. We were hoping to get him to ninety, but his body gave out. Fortunately, being my own boss at the time and with not much work to do thanks to COVID (and yes, glory to God for opening this window for me), I had the opportunity to spend some quality time with my dad before he died. During that time, I had a chance to awkwardly share the gospel with him. The last time I talked to him on the phone, he asked if I was still "into that religion thing" and going to church. I told him, "Absolutely, yes." He said that was great, it was a good thing for me.

A few days later, my sister Lisa called to say the end was close, and I should go to St. Louis and say goodbye. When I got to my Dad's apartment, he was essentially unresponsive. He never woke up for me, but I grabbed his hand and read him Psalm 40. He died just a few hours later. I will always be grateful to God for helping to make this moment happen—and showing me the path even when I didn't know there was a path to follow.

REFLECTION: THINK ABOUT THE HIGH PLACES IN YOUR LIFE.

1] What do you spend the most amount of time on Monday through Friday? On the weekends?

2] Can you identify what the high places are in your life? Do those high places lead to other sins?

3] What are two or three things you can do today to put God first in your life?

■ CHAPTER 7 ■

CANCELLING OF MY CULTURE - REBUILDING OF ME

"If you refuse to take up your cross and follow me, you are not worthy of being mine. If you cling to your life, you will lose it; but if you give up your life for me, you will find it."

—Matthew 10:38–39 NLT

March Madness. Those two words would normally bring an irrational giddiness to my step—and bring literal madness and misery to Amy. For millions of Americans, March means the annual celebration of college basketball, the NCAA hoops tournament bracket and the Final Four. For me, March Madness was something much more serious. This was a month-long holiday that I worshiped with as much zeal as I could possibly generate. Why?

My university's team, the Kansas Jayhawks, was usually considered one of the best in the nation, consistently playing until the final weekend of the month. All the excitement of the tournament meant multiple outings with my friends to join hundreds of other college hoops junkies at our favorite sports bar. Sometimes, I would get to the bar three or four hours early to hold a table for the group. And as I shared in the previous chapter, it always included drinking way too much. If Kansas University (KU) kept winning, the month just kept getting better and more exciting. If KU lost early in the month, my mood was destroyed for weeks.

The highlight of every March, though, took place right in downtown Kansas City—the Big 12 Men's Basketball Tournament. This event is scheduled for the start of the month, so it signifies the beginning of the "hoops holiday season" and the subsequent arrival of spring.

Every year, my group of friends made the pilgrimage to the Living Room in downtown Kansas City, which was basically a giant outdoor bar that was right across the street from the arena. Thousands of fans crammed into this space before and after every game. Since a large portion of the KU alumni base is in KC, we were surrounding by Jayhawk gear. Our group usually never went inside to watch the games because we preferred to stay outside and float along in the sea of humanity throughout the day. It was a sinners' paradise, and I led the parade.

March 2020 was shaping up to be an all-time celebration. KU was the clear number one team in the country and the prohibitive favorite to make the Final Four and win the national championship. But a week before the start of the Big 12 tournament in Kansas City, a troubling trend was bubbling. There was talk that COVID-19 was going to possibly derail March Madness, though we never really believed it. The Big 12 tournament was to start on Wednesday evening, with KU set to play during the day on Thursday. On the Monday prior, it was all systems go: the tournament was still scheduled to be played, and the excitement was building.

When Wednesday came, other leagues began cancelling their tournaments. While the Big 12 announced that the games would go on, no fans would be allowed. But our group would not be stopped. We were going to have our traditional Thursday at the Big 12 celebration, with or without COVID. We gathered as usual at 9:30 am for the annual shot-gunning of the beer before we walked over to the tournament.

When we got to the Living Room, instead of being inundated with fans, it was the five of us and about forty other people—truly a ghost town compared to previous years. As the morning went on, more and more games were getting cancelled. Finally, about thirty minutes before tip-off of the first game, the Big 12 pulled the plug on the tournament literally out from under our feet. Little did I know this would also be the moment the plug was pulled on my own culture.

> *Indeed, all who desire to live a godly life in Christ Jesus will be persecuted, while evil people and impostors will go on from bad to worse, deceiving and being deceived (2 Timothy 3:12–13 ESV).*

I think we are all familiar with the phrase "cancel culture" in today's world. A reputation that took decades to build can come crashing down in a matter of hours with just one poorly timed tweet or post on social media. If your opinion goes against the feelings of the mob, you are done. And it's not just celebrities getting cancelled these days. People who live their lives in relative anonymity face the real possibility of losing a career or a college scholarship by what they say. I am no fan of this rising cancel culture and those who use it for evil, but it can be used for good as well.

I experienced my own version of this once I unmasked my life, courtesy of God—and that's exactly the way it needed to be. As I shared over the course of this story, I was enslaved by the culture of this world no matter where I turned (sports, TV shows, movies, social media).

I was tempted to follow along with a worldview that focused on sex, pride, idolatry, and all the trappings that the man-made universe offers. I think back to all those MTV videos I watched at a teen, those R-rated movies that I had direct access to thanks to cable TV, the constant barrage of sex and violence. I know there are people who think "religion" brainwashed me. Well, what about the brainwashing I got watching television growing up? That absolutely skewed my view of women, sex, and our culture in general.

For the first forty-nine years of my life, I was completely content to go along with it. Frankly, I wasn't just content with today's culture, I reveled in it and glorified it. I celebrated it. It was *my culture*. The only way I was going to break free from the addiction of *my culture* and join *God's culture* was through divine intervention. That's exactly what happened.

Definition of CANCEL (verb):

To decide not to conduct or perform [something planned or expected] usually without expectation of conducting or performing it at a later time; or to destroy the force, effectiveness, or validity of

—Merriam-Webster (online), last updated May 8, 2021, https://www.merriam-webster.com/dictionary/cancel

Definition of CULTURE (noun):

The characteristic features of everyday existence [such as diversions or a way of life] shared by people in a place or time

—Merriam-Webster(online), last updated May 9, 2021, https://www.merriam-webster.com/dictionary/culture

If I was going to truly pick up my cross and walk away from my old ways of living, I needed to **DESTROY THE FORCE** of the everyday *diversions* in my life. I freely admit that I was not strong enough to do that on my own. I let God work His will through my heart, and the culture I worked so hard to hold on to lost its grip on my life. That cancellation of March Madness and sports in general in 2020 was really the beginning of how I was able to break free from those addictive behaviors in my life.

Every few weeks, Amy will ask me this question. "If Coronavirus didn't exist, do you think you would have changed your life?" That's a hard question for me to answer. Well, in actuality, no, it's not that hard to answer. Deep down, I know that without the pandemic shutting down life as I knew it, I would likely still be trapped in my sin and addictions. Fortunately, God had other plans, and I took advantage of a once-in-a-lifetime opportunity to start anew.

So how does one work on cancelling your own culture?

You must fill up your heart with God. When I say fill up on God, I literally mean filling up as much time during the day as you can thinking about the Lord, worshiping the Him, and seeking the Him. On that random Tuesday night when you have nothing to do, how are you filling up your time? Are you studying scripture or studying the fantasy football stats from last week? Are you "doom scrolling" your way through Twitter and Facebook, or are you listening to podcasts from your favorite preacher? Are you organizing your Netflix queue or trying to build a real relationship with God and His followers?

Here's how I started filling up my new heart:

I built a relationship with God. I read the Bible *every single day*. Seems rather obvious, but I was shocked that quite a few Christians often neglect the easiest way to know the voice of God. Pray every morning before you open Facebook and get your day started. Find times throughout the day to focus on God, even for just a few minutes at a time. The more you put into building a relationship with God, the more you will get out of it.

I put God at the center of all my other relationships. My marriage is so much stronger today than it ever has been. Why? God is in the middle of most things Amy and I do together. We spend time together at church, we get out of our comfort zone and meet new believers, and we watch spiritually-centered movies or TV shows. We have actual conversations about our beliefs. It took a while, but now we've both put God first in our lives and that's been the key to how we've been able to move beyond the sins of my past.

I replaced the "garbage" content of my life and started filling up on the good things that nourish my mind and soul. I had a lot of "reprogramming" to do in order to cancel my culture and build it back up with a focus on God. It's critical to remove the distractions in life that offer no nutrients. Fortunately, there is a lot of great content available in podcast form that will help fill your heart with the things of God. The four podcasts I can't live without include:

- The Bible Recap - This podcast offers a daily Bible reading plan and then helps you make sense of what you read with a daily, ten-minute recap show. This has helped expand my knowledge of the Bible immensely.

- The Alisa Childers podcast and The Bible Thinker podcast - These two shows were the first ones I found on my spiritual journey. They not only set out to answer questions from an apologetics evangelism point of view, but they also give me confidence in how I might answer those same questions as they come up in my own world.

- The Paul Tripp podcast - Outside of Phillip O'Reilly at my church, The Rock of KC, there is no pastor I want to listen to more than

Paul Tripp. He delivers powerful sermons that always seem to go directly to the heart problem of sin that all humans carry.

I went to church. I know that's been tough in the age of COVID, but having an opportunity to worship God with others is extremely gratifying. I had actually tried going to church when I was twenty-one around the time of the first Gulf War in Iraq. For those of us in Generation-X, this was our first real existential debate over war. Yes, we lived through the Cold War, but now this was an actual battlefield. So, I went to a nondenominational church thinking they wouldn't talk about Jesus, but I was a little off on that one—one time was enough. I also went to synagogue, but felt completely out of place and lost—once was enough there too. Thirty years later, Amy and I go to church on Saturday evenings. It's really a great way to get your mind right at the end of the week.

I read books about God. I mentioned Erwin McManus earlier and he's a great place to start, as he has several books that can feed you on your spiritual journey. For the baseball fans out there, I absolutely devoured Darryl Strawberry's testimony in *Turn Your Season Around*, a fascinating look at his own journey to Christ as a superstar athletic figure. Find a book, load it on your phone, start listening, and fuel your own curiosity.

I got off the couch and got physically active. It's just as important to work your body as it is to work your soul. And guess what? This makes it incredibly easy to read the Bible. I run on average six days a week, and on every run I listen to the Bible on my iPhone. There's not a greater emotional boost than finishing a run while listening to scripture. I actually finished listening to the entire Bible in six months that way. Now that is a miracle!

"If the world hates you, know that it has hated me before it hated you. If you were of the world, the world would love you as its own; but because you are not of the world, but I chose you out of the world, therefore the world hates you" (John 15:18–19 ESV).

Filling up on God was the easy part. I made sure that I was so focused on building a relationship with God that I didn't have time for any of those cultural distractions. But truly cancelling my old life takes a lot of patience and a lot of praying. You need to find ways to remove every ounce of temptation from your life.

It starts with *social media*. My kids used to tell me that I had FOMO (fear of missing out – I had to look that one up) if I wasn't scrolling through my social media accounts. I had become addicted to Facebook and Twitter because I didn't want to miss out on the latest breaking news, viral video, or celebrity scandal. It was the ultimate timewaster. The Bible tells us to be "quick to listen, slow to speak, and slow to become angry" (James 1:19 ESV). Social media tells us to share every single thought in your head and make sure to attack anyone you disagree with.

As my world view changed (and it has dramatically over the year), I noticed that nearly everyone I previously followed leaned left to heavy-left on the political spectrum. Despite all of that, the true reality for me is that social media was the ultimate temptation that led me to porn and infidelity. I needed to cut it out of my life, so I deleted my Twitter, Instagram, and Snapchat accounts. I'm still on Facebook but mainly for the birthdays reminders and getting updates from my homeowners' association. I do rely on Twitter's trending topics tab to stay updated on news, but since I no longer have an account, I can't post or interact with any users. I will be back on social media someday, but it will be as Neil, the follower of Jesus.

The next target on my cancel culture tour*: cable TV, Netflix, Hulu, and YouTubeTV*. I got rid of them all and never looked back. My cable company, Hulu and YouTubeTV kept adding channels I never asked for and have awful programming. In addition, they were raising their monthly subscription fees by twenty-five percent in some cases, which made it fairly easy to walk away. Netflix was the one I was hanging on to as long as I could.

Even though most of their programming was filled with sex and violence—things I just wanted no part of in my culture anymore—it still was home to my two favorite shows: *The Office* and *The Great British Baking Show*. I think I watched all nine seasons of The Office at least nine times, maybe more. That's part of the problem. Streaming services make it so easy to lose chunks of time binging on a show. Instead of focusing my time on building a relationship with God or talking with Amy, or engaging more with my kids, I stuffed my sins deep inside me and built a great one-way relationship with Michael Scott (a character from *The Office*). But again, God always seems to be looking out for me. *The Office* left Netflix for another streaming service at the end of 2020. I did not follow along and said "so long" to the gang at Dunder Mifflin (the fictional office setting).

As I mentioned above, God really deserves the credit for helping me break free from my sports fanaticism. What Amy failed to share about our first date in the introduction she wrote was that she asked me if I was a sports fanatic. I lied. If she knew the truth, I'm thinking she never would have started dating me. That's why it is so hard for me to explain the monumental change that happened in my life. I would watch sports nonstop, listen to people talk about sports on the car radio, read about sports, and attend sporting events every chance I could. To go from using sports as a coping mechanism from childhood to now watching as simply a form of entertainment like it was meant to be is amazing. Frankly, most people in my life would not be able to believe it; I still barely believe it myself.

Eliminating sports and pop culture entertainment from my diet made it easier to say goodbye to alcohol and marijuana. If I was out watching a game with my friends, there were multiple shots of whiskey involved. And Friday night was a lot more "fun" if I could "toke up" and "veg out" in front of *The Office* for three hours.

Most importantly, I haven't looked at pornography, been tempted to look at, or viewed any other images that might lead me to porn since April of 2020. With the power of God behind me, I know that my old life is gone forever. My culture has been officially cancelled.

I honestly thought I would miss all the mind-altering comforts my culture offered me, but I don't. I was trapped in a prison built out of my own sin. It was full of selfishness, deception, denial, depression, and darkness. Through the power of God, I broke away from the chains of my culture and was able to rebuild my life and restore the light I bring to the world. I have my freedom back.

> *"You are the light of the world. A town built on a hill cannot be hidden. Neither do people light a lamp and put it under a bowl. Instead they put it on its stand, and it gives light to everyone in the house. In the same way, let your light shine before others, that they may see your good deeds and glorify your Father in heaven" (Matthew 5:14–16 NIV).*

REFLECTION: THINK ABOUT THE CULTURE YOU LIVE IN.

1) What are some of the things you have in your culture that lead you to sin?

2) How do you spend your time during the week, and who do you spend it with? What about the weekends?

3) What are one or two things you can eliminate from your life today to help cancel your culture and the temptation in your life?

▪ CHAPTER 8 ▪

KEEPING THE MASK OFF FOREVER

"Fear not, for I am with you; be not dismayed, for I am your God; I will strengthen you, I will help you, I will uphold you with my righteous right hand."

—Isaiah 41:10 (ESV)

After a long battle to defeat the sin in my life, I willingly laid down my life and died on October 10, 2020. In a miracle that only God could create, I was reborn as a follower of Jesus just a few seconds later. My baptism capped off an amazing journey in 2020 that I still shake my head in disbelief over. We all have different seasons in our lives, and I think it is appropriate that I went through four of them in 2020 alone.

It started with the *Season of Sin* full of booze, porn, and infidelity. This wasn't really a new season as I had been in this cycle for a majority of my adult life. For those first three months of 2020, I did everything I could to keep my mask on and hold on to my sinful life, but those two souls in Chicago set me down this new path. Now I really want to send that couple a thank you note.

From there, it moved into a *Season of Suffering*. Facing a COVID-19 lockdown and having finally exposed my sin to Amy, I had to fully face all the harm and evil I brought into our marriage. There was literally nowhere to hide anymore. I couldn't leave Amy at home while I went and partied with my friends, trying my best to ignore the suffering I was creating in my home. But without having to face the misery, without being cut off from the world I wanted desperately to hang on to, there is no doubt I would still be trapped in my sin.

Once I did ask for God's help, it turned into a *Season of Faith*. I spent the summer building my relationship with God, reading the Bible, going to church, and investing as much time as could in Amy and my family. I know so many people lost loved ones in 2020; I lost my Dad. Yet I was still so blessed in this season. I am immensely grateful that I was in the position (partially thanks to COVID) to spend so much time with my

Dad before he died. I was able to share the Gospel with him and other members of my family as we took care of him (even though trying to talk to your Jewish mom about your new relationship with Jesus is awkward). That whole experience only accelerated my faith journey and brought me closer to God.

Closing 2020 and moving into a new year, I continue to be in a *Season of Rebirth.* By the grace of God, I have a new life here on Earth and a new life waiting for me in heaven once this life is over. Part of the rebirth is taking the mask off and exposing this new life to those who knew the old Neil. It's been shocking for those hearing my testimony, with a mixed reaction, honestly. Frankly, the Coronavirus lockdowns over the past year prevented me from telling more people, but I've made it my goal to share my story with as many people as possible in 2021 and beyond. If God can use my story to reach just one person with this book, it is a victory.

Pastor Phillip at The Rock of KC church shared in a sermon that COVID-19 was God's way of showing us what parts of our life need pruning. We should all take this opportunity to cut away the branches of our life that we don't need anymore: relationships, activities, social media, TV, or whatever sin you hold in your heart.

We need to remove those distractions and sins that pull us away from God, and let new branches take hold in our lives that draw us closer to Him. I nearly jumped out of my seat at church to yell a hearty "Amen" because those words resonated with me so completely. I do believe

COVID-19 came into the world to show us what we need and what we don't need. If you haven't already, it's not too late to start pruning away the sins from your life, leaving room for the good stuff to grow.

If I had to sum up how I plan to keep the good things growing in my life, these highlights from over the course of this book are the starting point. It's how I'm trying to keep my mask off, make my marriage healthy, and restore the bond I want with my sons and in all my relationships. I'm hopeful the light shining out of my broken heart can light a path for you as you reflect on the lessons God shared with me on my journey.

- **Start with God first.** I know this sounds like a broken record, but for me, none of this was possible without first asking for God's help. It's not just getting the help and walking away—you've got to have a daily relationship with God. I'm still amazed that there are people who feel they are religious and yet have no relationship with God. I remember talking to a friend about how I was able to read the entire Bible over the course of six months. He admitted that he had gone to church his whole life but probably read no more than ten pages of the Bible. Change your relationship with God and it will change your life.

- **Be open and honest in your relationships.** This continues to be a tough one for me as the shame and feelings of being alone I battled my entire life often make me choke on my own words. In my professional life I help put words in other peoples' mouths, but in my personal life I keep my feelings bottled up until they burst out of me. That's not healthy for me, and it's not healthy for my relationships—especially with Amy. While I was comfortable in my own silence, I realized that it was a source of anxiety for Amy.

That apprehension she had only grew once I took off my mask and admitted my sins. It would make Amy question my motives if I didn't share all my thoughts and feelings with her. I'm making progress, and the honest conversations we now have serve as a great foundation for rebuilding our marriage.

- **Spend time together.** I feel like this is an easy box to check for most men, but it wasn't for me. I would spend more time with work, friends, or sports than my wife. That's not a marriage. We committed early on to have consistent date nights. Once a week we would go do something and focus on being a couple. It was a bit tougher to do in a pandemic, but we managed. Some weeks it was dinner, others it was church. Whatever it was, we had to be intentional about doing it. Just as important, instead of talking about the deep issues we were working on, we would spend a lot of dates simply learning about each other again.

- **Forgiveness.** This story is not possible without Amy forgiving me for my sins. And if Amy can forgive me for my acts, I *promise* you can forgive your partner for not doing the laundry, not taking out the trash, or not fixing whatever might be wrong with the house. But I also had to learn that forgiveness doesn't mean there are no consequences. Amy might have forgiven me, but it doesn't take away the pain and hurt that I caused. Once I was able to realize this, it gave me the patience I needed to let Amy not only forgive but also get angry about what happened. She has earned the right to ask the tough questions and get the full answers she wants without me getting defensive.

- **Turn your life into an open book.** It is amazing what taking off your mask can do for your life. I was so trapped by my sins that it took every ounce of energy in my body and brain to hide them from Amy. I was so consumed and distracted with keeping those secrets masked that I had no time to think about anything else, much less try to engage in a conversation with Amy or my kids. Take the mask of your life off and live in freedom—no more angst and no more anxiety.

- **Identify your high places and work to remove them from your life.** We all have sins that we deal with, and this world we live in offers way too many distractions. It is imperative for us to get and stay focused on what's most important, that relationship with God I keep referring to. Identify those high places, big and small, and work on how you can prune them out of your life. I guarantee you will not miss those things at all. In fact, they will be replaced with the nourishment your soul needs.

- **Be aware of your culture and avoid temptation.** I know I am a sinner and there is a giant target on my back for the enemy to take aim. It is essential that I am always aware of my surroundings to avoid the temptation that's going to lead me down the wrong path. It's not only important to identify and remove your high places, but you've got to keep an eye on those negative influences in your life. Maybe that's in the form of the movies or TV shows you watch. Maybe it's that sporting event that takes you down to the bar. Or is it a website that slyly pushes you on your path toward porn? Whatever it is, the enemy is looking for ways to tempt you to sin. Cancel your own culture.

- **Break the cycle that haunts you.** For me, it was shame that was rooted deep in my childhood that plagued me into adulthood. The more I learned about the evils of pornography over the past year, the more I realized how it is often tied to something traumatic that happens to people as young kids. Find that source for you. I'm not a professional counselor, but I'm advising you not to walk but *run* to someone who you trust and can talk with to help you break whatever cycle is causing you to sin. That was key for me.

- **Find someone to walk the journey with you.** Obviously, Amy has become my rock through my journey, but it was also important to find others to encourage us along the way. The people of The Rock of KC Church have been a blessing. They opened their arms and church to us fully, inspire us, love us for who we are, and have become our family. Now we are amazed to see how our own story is inspiring others in our church.

- **Love your neighbor.** I shared the passage from Mark 12 in chapter 6 where Jesus told us to love God first and love your neighbor second. These are the two most important commandments to follow. I shared this verse in particular because there is too much hate and judgement in the world today. We all need to do a better job in taking care of our neighbors and lifting each other up. I think about the sin in my life and how it dishonors God, Amy, my boys, my family, and my friends, but I also know that my sin hurts all my fellow human beings as well. I've contributed my share of hate in this world, so I continue to be humbled by God for His mercy and forgiveness.

Back in chapter 1, I questioned if Amy would ever be able to see the new me. I finally know the answer. Yes, she can. It's taken a lot of patience and innumerable conversations, but we overhauled and rebuilt our marriage. We finally have the relationship we both wanted when we got married nearly ten years ago. Of course, that doesn't mean that we still do not have difficult conversations or that the past is completely behind us. It's not.

There are times when I'm being overly quiet or in a down mood, and that will trigger Amy to fear that I am shutting down and hiding something. That anxiety will cause her to go through every app on my phone just to make sure the evil hasn't returned. I know that's a fear Amy is going to have to deal with forever. That's why God is at the center of all we do. Our faith journey continues today, together. Amy and I remain a work in progress and will likely stay that way until the day we leave this earth. But there's no doubt that we have both learned important lessons about how to keep our marriage strong.

The overwhelming majority of days are good days. Here's a great example of some of the good ones. It was Thanksgiving weekend, about eight-months removed from that fateful text in the night from Chicago. Amy and I spent the holiday at my sister's house in St. Louis while our boys were spending Thanksgiving with their other respective parental units. We stayed in a bed-and-breakfast in Rocheport, MO on the way back home Friday night, about halfway between St. Louis and KC. I'd say it was the best night we had spent together since my unmasking—no outside distractions, a wonderful dinner at a local restaurant, an awesome attic room, and just us. A wonderful opportunity to focus on ourselves.

We got back to KC on Saturday in time to hit the weekend church service and fill up on God. That night, while searching for a movie to watch, we landed on *The Case for Christ*. It's about the true story of an atheist reporter, Lee Strobel, who set out to prove that Jesus wasn't real. Instead of proving that, he in fact found his own faith. I don't know why but that hit me right in the "feels." Obviously, I can relate to going from atheism to discovering God, but I could also relate to the struggles Lee had with his own wife, who was a believer.

Once the movie ended, Amy and I looked at each and we both just started sobbing, because I think we both realized at that moment just how blessed we were. It was the best cry I had in my entire life. On Sunday, it was a day of relaxing and spending more time together. It was a simple weekend, and one I will cherish forever. It was a weekend I didn't think was possible at the start of the year.

Trying to recall all the worst moments in my life that led me to committing some truly offensive acts often induces the sensation I get when I hear fingernails on a chalkboard. Writing this book has been a series of cringe-worthy, head-in-my-hands recollections. It's also given me a unique opportunity to demonstrate the healing power of God.

In the parable of healing the blind man in John 9, Jesus told the beggar, "As long as I am in the world, I am the light of the world" (John 9:5 ESV). After that, Jesus anointed the man's eyes with mud and suddenly, the man trapped in blindness his whole life, could finally see the light. But instead of marveling at the miracle of this man being rescued from a life of darkness, the pharisees questioned how it was even possible. I love how the man responded.

"Why, this is an amazing thing! You do not know where he comes from, and yet he opened my eyes. We know that God does not listen to sinners, but if anyone is a worshiper of God and does his will, God listens to him. Never since the world began has it been heard that anyone opened the eyes of a man born blind. If this man were not from God, he could do nothing" (John 9:30–33 ESV).

I hope you see that good news in my story. I was absolutely the biggest sinner in the world. I was spiritually blind and trapped in my own darkness. Jesus healed my blindness, and God still welcomed me home with open arms. He never turned His back on me even though I tried running away from Him every chance I could. If you are struggling with addiction, depression, anxiety, or just focused too much on the sins of this world, there is a way to take off that mask and walk in the path of a new life. I'm one of God's miracles. If you know someone going through a season of suffering, be patient, pray, and forgive.

REFLECTION: THINK ABOUT THE PAST YEAR OF YOUR LIFE.

1] What are the areas of your life you need to prune?

2] What are one or two new ways you can fill up your personal time with positive activities?

3] How are you going to strengthen the relationship you have with God going forward?

4] How are you going to use your faith to strengthen your relationship with your spouse and family?

Here's my prayer for you, my dear reader. I appreciate you. And I love you.

Father, thank You for the new life You have given me. I was dead in my sin until You rescued me. I will be forever grateful for Your mercy and forgiveness. I ask that You work Your will through the people reading this story. Father, soften their hearts so they can receive the Good News, turn away from their sinful life, pick up their own cross, and follow Jesus. Amen.